11+
Verbal Reasoning
GL & Other Styles

WORKBOOK 5

Additional Multiple-choice Practice Questions

Dr Stephen C Curran

Edited by Andrea Richardson & Nell Bond

This book belongs to

ae
PUBLICATIONS

Accelerated Education Publications Ltd

Contents

Chapter Twenty-six
SIMILAR MEANINGS

In these questions, find **one** word from **each** group that are closest in meaning. Choose **both** words from the options provided.

Example:

(boring   standard   exciting)
(normal   different   nice)

standard
normal

1. Level One

Exercise 26: 1   Write the two words that are closest in meaning:

Score

1) **(mild   make   mend)**
   (repair   recent   retire)

   a) **mild**   b) **make**   c) **mend**   d) **repair**   e) **recent**   f) **retire**

2) **(gust   goal   grow)**
   (arm   aim   arc)

   a) **gust**   b) **goal**   c) **grow**   d) **arm**   e) **aim**   f) **arc**

3) **(link   lose   lull)**
   (bend   bell   bond)

   a) **link**   b) **lose**   c) **lull**   d) **bend**   e) **bell**   f) **bond**

4) **(hope   heap   hips)**
   (stack   shops   short)

   a) **hope**   b) **heap**   c) **hips**   d) **stack**   e) **shops**   f) **short**

5) **(same   some   ship)**
   (along   alike   about)

   a) **same**   b) **some**   c) **ship**   d) **along**   e) **alike**   f) **about**

6) (open once over)   _____
   (angel anger above)   _____

   a) open   b) once   c) over   d) angel   e) anger   f) above

7) (ails arch area)   _____
   (curve couch caves)   _____

   a) ails   b) arch   c) area   d) curve   e) couch   f) caves

8) (gasp gone gain)   _____
   (grip grow glow)   _____

   a) gasp   b) gone   c) gain   d) grip   e) grow   f) glow

9) (fall foal fine)   _____
   (dome drop done)   _____

   a) fall   b) foal   c) fine   d) dome   e) drop   f) done

10) (zone zinc zero)   _____
    (nun nut nil)   _____

    a) zone   b) zinc   c) zero   d) nun   e) nut   f) nil

11) (sink swat sure)   _____
    (hit hot hat)   _____

    a) sink   b) swat   c) sure   d) hit   e) hot   f) hat

12) (hart hare help)   _____
    (aim arm aid)   _____

    a) hart   b) hare   c) help   d) aim   e) arm   f) aid

13) (pick port pole)   _____
    (rest reap road)   _____

    a) pick   b) port   c) pole   d) rest   e) reap   f) road

4

14) **(knot kind kite)**   _____
     (boat blue bind)   _____
       a) **knot**   b) **kind**   c) **kite**   d) **boat**   e) **blue**   f) **bind**

15) **(hers head hero)**   _____
     (idol idea into)   _____
       a) **hers**   b) **head**   c) **hero**   d) **idol**   e) **idea**   f) **into**

16) **(lack lane leap)**   _____
     (noun need nice)   _____
       a) **lack**   b) **lane**   c) **leap**   d) **noun**   e) **need**   f) **nice**

17) **(rope risk rate)**   _____
     (danger dancer dental)   _____
       a) **rope**   b) **risk**   c) **rate**   d) **danger**   e) **dancer**   f) **dental**

18) **(teeth storm actual)**   _____
     (real false cloud)   _____
       a) **teeth**   b) **storm**   c) **actual**   d) **real**   e) **false**   f) **cloud**

19) **(tale tool tail)**   _____
     (shake story smart)   _____
       a) **tale**   b) **tool**   c) **tail**   d) **shake**   e) **story**   f) **smart**

20) **(soft song solo)**   _____
     (alone aware aside)   _____
       a) **soft**   b) **song**   c) **solo**   d) **alone**   e) **aware**   f) **aside**

2. Level Two

Exercise 26: 2   Write the two words that are closest in meaning: Score

1) **(day brave horse)**   _____
   (knight timid bold)   _____
     a) **day**   b) **brave**   c) **horse**   d) **knight**   e) **timid**   f) **bold**

2) **(happy   emotion   messy)**　_____
   (chaotic   neat   tired)　_____

   a) **happy**   b) **emotion**   c) **messy**   d) **chaotic**   e) **neat**   f) **tired**

3) **(rare   typical   timber)**　_____
   (dwelling   build   usual)　_____

   a) **rare**   b) **typical**   c) **timber**   d) **dwelling**   e) **build**   f) **usual**

4) **(cheerful   whine   utter)**　_____
   (grapes   voice   complain)　_____

   a) **cheerful**   b) **whine**   c) **utter**   d) **grapes**   e) **voice**   f) **complain**

5) **(want   wait   wilt)**　_____
   (dream   dames   droop)　_____

   a) **want**   b) **wait**   c) **wilt**   d) **dream**   e) **dames**   f) **droop**

6) **(glass   nudge   avid)**　_____
   (polish   bump   avoid)　_____

   a) **glass**   b) **nudge**   c) **avid**   d) **polish**   e) **bump**   f) **avoid**

7) **(corrode   recite   repute)**　_____
   (respite   cornice   narrate)　_____

   a) **corrode**   b) **recite**   c) **repute**   d) **respite**   e) **cornice**   f) **narrate**

8) **(faith   church   honest)**　_____
   (lies   altar   belief)　_____

   a) **faith**   b) **church**   c) **honest**   d) **lies**   e) **altar**   f) **belief**

9) **(cow   plant   garden)**　_____
   (sow   tree   animal)　_____

   a) **cow**   b) **plant**   c) **garden**   d) **sow**   e) **tree**   f) **animal**

10) **(sign   male   cancel)** _____
    (start   stop   post) _____

    a) **sign**   b) **male**   c) **cancel**   d) **start**   e) **stop**   f) **post**

11) **(devoid   normal   gadget)** _____
    (strange   germ   device) _____

    a) **devoid**   b) **normal**   c) **gadget**   d) **strange**   e) **germ**   f) **device**

12) **(chorus   din   church)** _____
    (music   note   choir) _____

    a) **chorus**   b) **din**   c) **church**   d) **music**   e) **note**   f) **choir**

13) **(wary   wreck   new)** _____
    (ruin   ship   ancient) _____

    a) **wary**   b) **wreck**   c) **new**   d) **ruin**   e) **ship**   f) **ancient**

14) **(water   chute   baby)** _____
    (slide   shoot   cute) _____

    a) **water**   b) **chute**   c) **baby**   d) **slide**   e) **shoot**   f) **cute**

15) **(midst   ending   final)** _____
    (clear   foggy   middle) _____

    a) **midst**   b) **ending**   c) **final**   d) **clear**   e) **foggy**   f) **middle**

16) **(pint   industry   unify)** _____
    (separate   merge   unit) _____

    a) **pint**   b) **industry**   c) **unify**   d) **separate**   e) **merge**   f) **unit**

17) **(theme   bounty   tropic)** _____
    (palm   beech   topic) _____

    a) **theme**   b) **bounty**   c) **tropic**   d) **palm**   e) **beech**   f) **topic**

18) **(ability   clone   blame)** _____
    (useless   talent   compete) _____

   a) **ability**   b) **clone**   c) **blame**   d) **useless**   e) **talent**   f) **compete**

19) **(police   energy   sun)** _____
    (friction   solar   force) _____

   a) **police**   b) **energy**   c) **sun**   d) **friction**   e) **solar**   f) **force**

20) **(dismay   calm   happy)** _____
    (shock   clam   studious) _____

   a) **dismay**   b) **calm**   c) **happy**   d) **shock**   e) **clam**   f) **studious**

3. Level Three

Exercise 26: 3   Write the two words that are closest   **Score**
in meaning:

1) **(sparse   rouble   debris)** _____
   (euro   rubble   plenty) _____

   a) **sparse**   b) **rouble**   c) **debris**
   d) **euro**   e) **rubble**   f) **plenty**

2) **(emergency   patent   patient)** _____
   (tolerant   impatient   hospital) _____

   a) **emergency**   b) **patent**   c) **patient**
   d) **tolerant**   e) **impatient**   f) **hospital**

3) **(scene   cosmos   planet)** _____
   (orbit   vista   play) _____

   a) **scene**   b) **cosmos**   c) **planet**
   d) **orbit**   e) **vista**   f) **play**

4) **(measure   exact   accurate)**
   (guess   gauge   height)   _____
                                          _____

   a) **measure**   b) **exact**   c) **accurate**
   d) **guess**   e) **gauge**   f) **height**

5) **(possess   possible   diploma)**
   (unlikely   dilemma   probable)   _____
                                          _____

   a) **possess**   b) **possible**   c) **diploma**
   d) **unlikely**   e) **dilemma**   f) **probable**

6) **(decisive   derivative   significant)**
   (important   insignificant   desire)   _____
                                          _____

   a) **decisive**   b) **derivative**   c) **significant**
   d) **important**   e) **insignificant**   f) **desire**

7) **(tyranny   tyre   tyrant)**
   (diction   dictator   diphthong)   _____
                                          _____

   a) **tyranny**   b) **tyre**   c) **tyrant**
   d) **diction**   e) **dictator**   f) **diphthong**

8) **(courteous   dampen   rude)**
   (fruit   cordial   drink)   _____
                                          _____

   a) **courteous**   b) **dampen**   c) **rude**
   d) **fruit**   e) **cordial**   f) **drink**

9) **(jealous   garish   sombre)**
   (delight   envious   futile)   _____
                                          _____

   a) **jealous**   b) **garish**   c) **sombre**
   d) **delight**   e) **envious**   f) **futile**

10) **(freight   fragrant   fragment)**
    (aromatic   aura   stench)   _____
                                          _____

    a) **freight**   b) **fragrant**   c) **fragment**
    d) **aromatic**   e) **aura**   f) **stench**

Chapter Twenty-seven
WORD LINKS

In these questions there are two pairs of words. One of the five answers will go **equally well** with **both** pairs of words. Choose the word from the options provided.

Example:

(mail   letter)

(pole   stake)   Answer: _____*post*_____

a) **stick**   b) **parcel**   c) **gamble**   d) **post**   e) **half**

1. Level One

Exercise 27: 1   Find the word that will go with both pairs of words:

Score

1) **(quick   fast)**

(cold   chilly)   Answer: _____

a) **freezing**   b) **patch**   c) **nippy**   d) **rapid**   e) **issue**

2) **(squeeze   nip)**

(steal   take)   Answer: _____

a) **pinch**   b) **unity**   c) **total**   d) **thieve**   e) **twist**

3) **(cultivate   grow)**

(ranch   smallholding)   Answer: _____

a) **wages**   b) **farm**   c) **verse**   d) **garage**   e) **usage**

4) **(residence   dwelling)**

(lodge   board)   Answer: _____

a) **stay**   b) **whole**   c) **stone**   d) **house**   e) **store**

5) **(best top)**
   (idol celebrity)   Answer: _____
   a) **miles**   b) **champion**   c) **teams**   d) **voice**   e) **star**

6) **(lock secure)**
   (join connect)   Answer: _____
   a) **trap**   b) **shine**   c) **touch**   d) **fasten**   e) **shut**

7) **(permit agree)**
   (donation award)   Answer: _____
   a) **argue**   b) **allow**   c) **grant**   d) **happy**   e) **plump**

8) **(stain smudge)**
   (place location)   Answer: _____
   a) **sandy**   b) **spot**   c) **wine**   d) **piece**   e) **soil**

9) **(font script)**
   (pattern design)   Answer: _____
   a) **poach**   b) **style**   c) **march**   d) **print**   e) **legal**

10) **(more extra)**
    (advance extend)   Answer: _____
    a) **parent**   b) **moist**   c) **addition**   d) **purse**   e) **further**

11) **(squash cordial)**
    (liquid fluid)   Answer: _____
    a) **hoped**   b) **juice**   c) **irons**   d) **water**   e) **gully**

12) **(input enter)**
    (important main)   Answer: _____
    a) **start**   b) **send**   c) **key**   d) **chart**   e) **rest**

13) **(task   chore)**
    (work   occupation)   Answer: _____
      a) **dot**   b) **errand**   c) **guild**   d) **job**   e) **great**

14) **(smash   destroy)**
    (vacation   holiday)   Answer: _____
      a) **ruin**   b) **revise**   c) **break**   d) **change**   e) **alter**

15) **(choose   select)**
    (gather   harvest)   Answer: _____
      a) **twig**   b) **feel**   c) **pick**   d) **collect**   e) **fuse**

16) **(cover   shield)**
    (hue   tint)   Answer: _____
      a) **gaunt**   b) **hide**   c) **exist**   d) **shade**   e) **dwell**

17) **(type   kind)**
    (arrange   separate)   Answer: _____
      a) **play**   b) **sort**   c) **collate**   d) **fire**   e) **dove**

18) **(path   road)**
    (follow   chase)   Answer: _____
      a) **spy**   b) **flute**   c) **girth**   d) **flock**   e) **track**

19) **(carnival   circus)**
    (just   reasonable)   Answer: _____
      a) **hint**   b) **fair**   c) **knot**   d) **equal**   e) **maid**

20) **(penalty   charge)**
    (delicate   flimsy)   Answer: _____
      a) **fort**   b) **inch**   c) **fine**   d) **heat**   e) **fee**

2. Level Two

Exercise 27: 2   Find the word that will go with both pairs of words:

1) **(withdraw   recoil)**
   (sanctuary   refuge)   Answer: _____

   a) **house**   b) **happen**   c) **guilty**   d) **retreat**   e) **dodge**

2) **(feat   activity)**
   (abuse   manipulate)   Answer: _____

   a) **achieve**   b) **force**   c) **accomplish**   d) **control**   e) **exploit**

3) **(crash   bump)**
   (walkout   stoppage)   Answer: _____

   a) **riot**   b) **strike**   c) **hustle**   d) **bang**   e) **thump**

4) **(riddle   brainteaser)**
   (bewilder   confuse)   Answer: _____

   a) **muddle**   b) **quiz**   c) **trust**   d) **puzzle**   e) **quest**

5) **(costume   outfit)**
   (regular   identical)   Answer: _____

   a) **normal**   b) **uniform**   c) **proud**   d) **usual**   e) **dress**

6) **(intend   propose)**
   (drawing   chart)   Answer: _____

   a) **plied**   b) **instant**   c) **fluent**   d) **plan**   e) **sketch**

7) **(current   existing)**
   (gift   offering)   Answer: _____

   a) **present**   b) **inspect**   c) **poster**   d) **souvenir**   e) **reward**

8) **(store hoard)**
   (substitute extra)   Answer: _____

   a) **spare**   b) **accumulate**   c) **reserve**   d) **arrive**   e) **drawer**

9) **(energy sparkle)**
   (existence being)   Answer: _____

   a) **survive**   b) **individual**   c) **affirm**   d) **life**   e) **enthusiasm**

10) **(buy sell)**
    (pact treaty)   Answer: _____

    a) **package**   b) **deal**   c) **purchase**   d) **ideal**   e) **vend**

11) **(basin bowl)**
    (fall descend)   Answer: _____

    a) **bath**   b) **wharf**   c) **drop**   d) **viral**   e) **sink**

12) **(fling toss)**
    (confuse baffle)   Answer: _____

    a) **cover**   b) **throw**   c) **shoot**   d) **mystify**   e) **noble**

13) **(last continue)**
    (suffer tolerate)   Answer: _____

    a) **bear**   b) **triumph**   c) **endure**   d) **latest**   e) **experience**

14) **(learn revise)**
    (report review)   Answer: _____

    a) **study**   b) **single**   c) **render**   d) **story**   e) **account**

15) **(slab wedge)**
    (barricade impede)   Answer: _____

    a) **police**   b) **trap**   c) **piece**   d) **tremor**   e) **block**

16) **(nasty unkind)**
   (imply convey)   Answer: _____
   a) **heartless** b) **leads** c) **guest** d) **frill** e) **mean**

17) **(arena ground)**
   (sway lurch)   Answer: _____
   a) **swagger** b) **stadium** c) **abide** d) **pitch** e) **earth**

18) **(protest complain)**
   (entity article)   Answer: _____
   a) **dispute** b) **particle** c) **gripe** d) **warble** e) **object**

19) **(drive ambition)**
   (power strength)   Answer: _____
   a) **authority** b) **steel** c) **force** d) **career** e) **control**

20) **(match parallel)**
   (even uniform)   Answer: _____
   a) **balance** b) **equal** c) **straight** d) **blazer** e) **pair**

3. Level Three

Exercise 27: 3   Find the word that will go with both pairs of words:

Score

1) **(pelt fleece)**
   (cover bury)   Answer: _____
   a) **conceal** b) **hide** c) **grave** d) **blanket** e) **wrap**

2) **(watch observe)**
   (display screen)   Answer: _____
   a) **timepiece** b) **exhibit** c) **scrutinize** d) **survey** e) **monitor**

3) **(advertise promote)**
   (bazaar souk)   Answer: _____

   a) **presentation**   b) **market**   c) **present**
   d) **magazine**   e) **superstore**

4) **(bunting banner)**
   (highlight identify)   Answer: _____

   a) **barrier**   b) **recognise**   c) **flag**   d) **advert**   e) **underline**

5) **(show exhibit)**
   (parade spectacle)   Answer: _____

   a) **procession**   b) **theatre**   c) **march**   d) **reveal**   e) **display**

6) **(present suggest)**
   (surrender accept)   Answer: _____

   a) **propose**   b) **submit**   c) **advise**   d) **defeat**   e) **abolish**

7) **(hovel dump)**
   (cavity hollow)   Answer: _____

   a) **tip**   b) **hole**   c) **warren**   d) **stench**   e) **crater**

8) **(loving caring)**
   (proposal submission)   Answer: _____

   a) **devoted**   b) **application**   c) **suggestion**
   d) **tender**   e) **adoration**

9) **(form figure)**
   (influence affect)   Answer: _____

   a) **class**   b) **number**   c) **involve**   d) **manipulate**   e) **shape**

10) **(fasten attach)**
    (direction approach)   Answer: _____

    a) **unite**   b) **route**   c) **tack**   d) **advance**   e) **bond**

Chapter Twenty-eight
OPPOSITE MEANINGS

In each question, find the **two** words, one from each group, that have the most **opposite** meaning. Choose **both** words from the options provided.

Example:

(up run walk)	up
(smile laugh down)	down

1. Level One

Exercise 28: 1   Find the two words that have the most opposite meaning:

Score

1) **(might alike laugh)** _____
   (glamorous thankful different) _____

   a) **might**   b) **alike**   c) **laugh**
   d) **glamorous**   e) **thankful**   f) **different**

2) **(frail leapt match)** _____
   (moist strong least) _____

   a) **frail**   b) **leapt**   c) **match**   d) **moist**   e) **strong**   f) **least**

3) **(knack laird fluid)** _____
   (solid leave juice) _____

   a) **knack**   b) **laird**   c) **fluid**   d) **solid**   e) **leave**   f) **juice**

4) **(melt fork hand)** _____
   (thread freeze starry) _____

   a) **melt**   b) **fork**   c) **hand**   d) **thread**   e) **freeze**   f) **starry**

5) **(sale bald bold)** _____
   (laced large hairy) _____

   a) **sale**   b) **bald**   c) **bold**   d) **laced**   e) **large**   f) **hairy**

6) **(leafy manor inner)** _____
   (frill outer gauge) _____

   a) **leafy**   b) **manor**   c) **inner**   d) **frill**   e) **outer**   f) **gauge**

7) **(hatch worst joint)** _____
   (best hunch grand) _____

   a) **hatch**   b) **worst**   c) **joint**   d) **best**   e) **hunch**   f) **grand**

8) **(plain heart image)** _____
   (fresh erupt fancy) _____

   a) **plain**   b) **heart**   c) **image**   d) **fresh**   e) **erupt**   f) **fancy**

9) **(frogs glare clean)** _____
   (empire soiled drowsy) _____

   a) **frogs**   b) **glare**   c) **clean**   d) **empire**   e) **soiled**   f) **drowsy**

10) **(lunch push mirth)** _____
    (pull flip cure) _____

    a) **lunch**   b) **push**   c) **mirth**   d) **pull**   e) **flip**   f) **cure**

11) **(rage chop fear)** _____
    (done calm bail) _____

    a) **rage**   b) **chop**   c) **fear**   d) **done**   e) **calm**   f) **bail**

12) **(learn glory pause)** _____
    (caravan continue bravest) _____
    a) **learn** b) **glory** c) **pause** d) **caravan** e) **continue** f) **bravest**

13) **(bring rapid chart)** _____
    (home slow hint) _____
    a) **bring** b) **rapid** c) **chart** d) **home** e) **slow** f) **hint**

14) **(decline offer dared)** _____
    (accept devote earned) _____
    a) **decline** b) **offer** c) **dared** d) **accept** e) **devote** f) **earned**

15) **(hold tale mist)** _____
    (factory release embrace) _____
    a) **hold** b) **tale** c) **mist** d) **factory** e) **release** f) **embrace**

16) **(enter gable rough)** _____
    (gift soft time) _____
    a) **enter** b) **gable** c) **rough** d) **gift** e) **soft** f) **time**

17) **(home fact book)** _____
    (number parking fiction) _____
    a) **home** b) **fact** c) **book** d) **number** e) **parking** f) **fiction**

18) **(wrong magic honey)** _____
    (bespoke correct award) _____
    a) **wrong** b) **magic** c) **honey** d) **bespoke** e) **correct** f) **award**

19) **(grunt hound level)** _____
    (uneven dainty dancer) _____
    a) **grunt** b) **hound** c) **level** d) **uneven** e) **dainty** f) **dancer**

20) (metal divide guide) _____

(join silver ledge) _____

a) metal   b) divide   c) guide   d) join   e) silver   f) ledge

2. Level Two

Exercise 28: 2   Find the two words that have the most opposite meaning:

1) (curry last bland) _____

(latest warm spicy) _____

a) curry   b) last   c) bland
d) latest   e) warm   f) spicy

2) (acknowledge garden helper) _____

(gadget reject ignore) _____

a) acknowledge   b) garden   c) helper
d) gadget   e) reject   f) ignore

3) (ideal flawed emblem) _____

(regard respond perfect) _____

a) ideal   b) flawed   c) emblem
d) regard   e) respond   f) perfect

4) (earning devote excess) _____

(dedicate glowing shortage) _____

a) earning   b) devote   c) excess
d) dedicate   e) glowing   f) shortage

5) (vacant guard hired) _____

(occupied secure glossy) _____

a) vacant   b) guard   c) hired
d) occupied   e) secure   f) glossy

6) (enrage   shout   lashed)   _____
   (rampage   console   quiet)   _____

   a) enrage   b) shout   c) lashed
   d) rampage   e) console   f) quiet

7) (determine   thrive   kindly)   _____
   (deteriorate   caring   thrifty)   _____

   a) determine   b) thrive   c) kindly
   d) deteriorate   e) caring   f) thrifty

8) (discuss   reach   direct)   _____
   (achieve   talk   winding)   _____

   a) discuss   b) reach   c) direct
   d) achieve   e) talk   f) winding

9) (forget   talent   stride)   _____
   (memory   recall   lose)   _____

   a) forget   b) talent   c) stride
   d) memory   e) recall   f) lose

10) (colour   permit   bold)   _____
    (bright   shade   shy)   _____

    a) colour   b) permit   c) bold
    d) bright   e) shade   f) shy

11) (trivial   pestle   ordeal)   _____
    (miner   important   trial)   _____

    a) trivial   b) pestle   c) ordeal
    d) miner   e) important   f) trial

12) **(parade   upset   spare)**
     (comfort   display   extra)

   a) **parade**   b) **upset**   c) **spare**
   d) **comfort**   e) **display**   f) **extra**

13) **(general   treaty   mend)**
     (major   repair   specific)

   a) **general**   b) **treaty**   c) **mend**
   d) **major**   e) **repair**   f) **specific**

14) **(pare   useful   scarce)**
     (abundant   trim   valuable)

   a) **pare**   b) **useful**   c) **scarce**
   d) **abundant**   e) **trim**   f) **valuable**

15) **(comprise   humble   dispute)**
     (disguise   arrogant   quarrel)

   a) **comprise**   b) **humble**   c) **dispute**
   d) **disguise**   e) **arrogant**   f) **quarrel**

16) **(bored   thrive   board)**
     (elapse   prosper   interested)

   a) **bored**   b) **thrive**   c) **board**
   d) **elapse**   e) **prosper**   f) **interested**

17) **(fault   intact   upright)**
     (error   horizontal   granite)

   a) **fault**   b) **intact**   c) **upright**
   d) **error**   e) **horizontal**   f) **granite**

18) (clear   install   liberal)   _____

(opaque   mount   original)   _____

a) clear   b) install   c) liberal
d) opaque   e) mount   f) original

19) (least   cautious   thin)   _____

(slightest   dilute   reckless)   _____

a) least   b) cautious   c) thin
d) slightest   e) dilute   f) reckless

20) (gorge   notion   scorch)   _____

(parch   starve   idea)   _____

a) gorge   b) notion   c) scorch
d) parch   e) starve   f) idea

3. Level Three

Exercise 28: 3   Find the two words that have the most opposite meaning:

1) (sequel   overhaul   placate)   _____

(result   subtle   irritate)   _____

a) sequel   b) overhaul   c) placate
d) result   e) subtle   f) irritate

2) (exclusive   merge   vacate)   _____

(detach   joust   unique)   _____

a) exclusive   b) merge   c) vacate
d) detach   e) joust   f) unique

3) (developed   ancient   mystic)   _____

(spiritual   primitive   vague)   _____

a) developed   b) ancient   c) mystic
d) spiritual   e) primitive   f) vague

4) (elude   crevice   pure) _____

(contaminated   fracture   evade) _____

   a) elude   b) crevice   c) pure

   d) contaminated   e) fracture   f) evade

5) (diminish   hinder   liable) _____

(delay   prone   escalate) _____

   a) diminish   b) hinder   c) liable

   d) delay   e) prone   f) escalate

6) (trusting   discard   expose) _____

(gullible   retain   eject) _____

   a) trusting   b) discard   c) expose

   d) gullible   e) retain   f) eject

7) (mundane   establish   agency) _____

(exceptional   bureau   proclaim) _____

   a) mundane   b) establish   c) agency

   d) exceptional   e) bureau   f) proclaim

8) (resist   soothe   refrain) _____

(oppose   persist   comfort) _____

   a) resist   b) soothe   c) refrain

   d) oppose   e) persist   f) comfort

9) (solitary   demure   assign) _____

(sociable   shy   delegate) _____

   a) solitary   b) demure   c) assign

   d) sociable   e) shy   f) delegate

10) (abscond   hoard   crave) _____

(yearn   desert   jettison) _____

   a) abscond   b) hoard   c) crave

   d) yearn   e) desert   f) jettison

Chapter Twenty-nine
ODD ONES OUT

In these questions three of the five words are connected in some way. Choose the **two** words that **do not** go with the other three words from the options provided.

Example:

blue   shed   black   rat   yellow

shed and _rat_

1. Level One

Exercise 29: 1   Write the two words which do not fit in with the others: Score

1)   **orange   apple   purple   fruit   green**

_____ and _____

a) **orange**   b) **apple**   c) **purple**   d) **fruit**   e) **green**

2)   **transport   train   tram   travel   coach**

_____ and _____

a) **transport**   b) **train**   c) **tram**   d) **travel**   e) **coach**

3)   **village   town   council   visit   city**

_____ and _____

a) **village**   b) **town**   c) **council**   d) **visit**   e) **city**

4)   **climb   ladder   stair   higher   step**

_____ and _____

a) **climb**   b) **ladder**   c) **stair**   d) **higher**   e) **step**

5) **knee   joint   elbow   hip   body**

   _____ and _____

   a) **knee**   b) **joint**   c) **elbow**   d) **hip**   e) **body**

6) **gas   coal   fuel   liquid   petrol**

   _____ and _____

   a) **gas**   b) **coal**   c) **fuel**   d) **liquid**   e) **petrol**

7) **sprint   sport   compete   run   jog**

   _____ and _____

   a) **sprint**   b) **sport**   c) **compete**   d) **run**   e) **jog**

8) **shape   pentagon   triangle   sign   square**

   _____ and _____

   a) **shape**   b) **pentagon**   c) **triangle**   d) **sign**   e) **square**

9) **crossing   canary   bird   parrot   pelican**

   _____ and _____

   a) **crossing**   b) **canary**   c) **bird**   d) **parrot**   e) **pelican**

10) **badminton   tennis   drink   squash   racquet**

   _____ and _____

   a) **badminton**   b) **tennis**   c) **drink**   d) **squash**   e) **racquet**

11) **sock   hat   coat   shoe   slipper**

   _____ and _____

   a) **sock**   b) **hat**   c) **coat**   d) **shoe**   e) **slipper**

12) **plough   knife   spade   farm   fork**

_____ and _____

a) **plough**   b) **knife**   c) **spade**   d) **farm**   e) **fork**

13) **feel   taste   touch   sweet   smell**

_____ and _____

a) **feel**   b) **taste**   c) **touch**   d) **sweet**   e) **smell**

14) **small   mouse   little   thimble   tiny**

_____ and _____

a) **small**   b) **mouse**   c) **little**   d) **thimble**   e) **tiny**

15) **cloud   black   grey   weather   white**

_____ and _____

a) **cloud**   b) **black**   c) **grey**   d) **weather**   e) **white**

16) **rugby   union   football   league   cricket**

_____ and _____

a) **rugby**   b) **union**   c) **football**   d) **league**   e) **cricket**

17) **shell   bay   cove   cave   gulf**

_____ and _____

a) **shell**   b) **bay**   c) **cove**   d) **cave**   e) **gulf**

18) **room   wall   ceiling   space   floor**

_____ and _____

a) **room**   b) **wall**   c) **ceiling**   d) **space**   e) **floor**

19) **float   canoe   swim   kayak   dinghy**

_____ and _____

a) **float**   b) **canoe**   c) **swim**   d) **kayak**   e) **dinghy**

20) **oblong   lords   oval   triangle   survey**

_____ and _____

a) **oblong**   b) **lords**   c) **oval**   d) **triangle**   e) **survey**

2. Level Two

Exercise 29: 2   Write the two words which do not
fit in with the others: Score

1) **festival   harvest   gather   reap   deliver**

_____ and _____

a) **festival**   b) **harvest**   c) **gather**   d) **reap**   e) **deliver**

2) **almond   brazil   country   pelican   pecan**

_____ and _____

a) **almond**   b) **brazil**   c) **country**   d) **pelican**   e) **pecan**

3) **bonnet   weaken   exhaust   kick   boot**

_____ and _____

a) **bonnet**   b) **weaken**   c) **exhaust**   d) **kick**   e) **boot**

4) **ferry   ruler   liner   yacht   regatta**

_____ and _____

a) **ferry**   b) **ruler**   c) **liner**   d) **yacht**   e) **regatta**

5) **shirt   blouse   shorts   shoes   cardigan**

_____ and _____

a) **shirt**   b) **blouse**   c) **shorts**   d) **shoes**   e) **cardigan**

6) **chop   stick   join   bore   bond**

_____ and _____

a) **chop**   b) **stick**   c) **join**   d) **bore**   e) **bond**

7) **notice   sign   observe   spot   site**

_____ and _____

a) **notice**   b) **sign**   c) **observe**   d) **spot**   e) **site**

8) **cherry   swede   lemon   leek   kiwi**

_____ and _____

a) **cherry**   b) **swede**   c) **lemon**   d) **leek**   e) **kiwi**

9) **stop   red   amber   green   go**

_____ and _____

a) **stop**   b) **red**   c) **amber**   d) **green**   e) **go**

10) **steam   train   electric   power   diesel**

_____ and _____

a) **steam**   b) **train**   c) **electric**   d) **power**   e) **diesel**

11) **joint   mortice   muscle   strong   tendon**

_____ and _____

a) **joint**   b) **mortice**   c) **muscle**   d) **strong**   e) **tendon**

12) **album   collect   annual   yearly   anthology**

_____ and _____

a) **album**   b) **collect**   c) **annual**   d) **yearly**   e) **anthology**

13) **cygnet   colt   fawn   owlet   cub**

_____ and _____

a) **cygnet**   b) **colt**   c) **fawn**   d) **owlet**   e) **cub**

14) **peach   avocado   raspberry   grape   plum**

_____ and _____

a) **peach**   b) **avocado**   c) **raspberry**   d) **grape**   e) **plum**

15) **burrow   tunnel   channel   mine   belong**

_____ and _____

a) **burrow**   b) **tunnel**   c) **channel**   d) **mine**   e) **belong**

16) **world   cone   dice   cube   sphere**

_____ and _____

a) **world**   b) **cone**   c) **dice**   d) **cube**   e) **sphere**

17) **wren   robin   celebrity   starlet   starling**

_____ and _____

a) **wren**   b) **robin**   c) **celebrity**   d) **starlet**   e) **starling**

18) **skin   knife   pare   peel   hair**

_____ and _____

a) **skin**   b) **knife**   c) **pare**   d) **peel**   e) **hair**

19) **collar   jacket   cuff   blazer   lapel**

_____ and _____

a) **collar**   b) **jacket**   c) **cuff**   d) **blazer**   e) **lapel**

20) **hedge   broom   rake   garden   shovel**

_____ and _____

a) **hedge**   b) **broom**   c) **rake**   d) **garden**   e) **shovel**

3. Level Three

Exercise 29: 3   Write the two words which do not fit in with the others:

Score

1) **elation   touch   feeling   sense   emotion**

_____ and _____

a) **elation**   b) **touch**   c) **feeling**   d) **sense**   e) **emotion**

2) **brusque   blunt   swift   hasty   curt**

_____ and _____

a) **brusque**   b) **blunt**   c) **swift**   d) **hasty**   e) **curt**

3) **trout   salmon   maroon   orange   banana**

_____ and _____

a) **trout**   b) **salmon**   c) **maroon**   d) **orange**   e) **banana**

4) **porpoise   octopus   dolphin   shark   whale**

_____ and _____

a) **porpoise**   b) **octopus**   c) **dolphin**   d) **shark**   e) **whale**

5) **canal   delta   accurate   estuary   strait**

_____ and _____

a) **canal**   b) **delta**   c) **accurate**   d) **estuary**   e) **strait**

6) **loam   decay   compost   mulch   ample**

_____ and _____

a) **loam**   b) **decay**   c) **compost**   d) **mulch**   e) **ample**

7) **canyon   gorge   summit   valley   oasis**

_____ and _____

a) **canyon**   b) **gorge**   c) **summit**   d) **valley**   e) **oasis**

8) **cabbage   parsnip   pumpkin   turnip   swede**

_____ and _____

a) **cabbage**   b) **parsnip**   c) **pumpkin**   d) **turnip**   e) **swede**

9) **direct   just   proper   right   almost**

_____ and _____

a) **direct**   b) **just**   c) **proper**   d) **right**   e) **almost**

10) **bogus   counterfeit   imitate   pretend   phoney**

_____ and _____

a) **bogus**   b) **counterfeit**   c) **imitate**   d) **pretend**   e) **phoney**

Chapter Thirty
MISSING WORDS

In these sentences, the word in capitals has had three letters next to each other taken out. Find the three letters and put them back into the word without changing their order. Choose the correct three-letter word from the options provided.

Example:

He was **ALS** well behaved.   AL**WAY**S

a) **WAY**   b) **SAY**   c) **YES**   d) **ONE**   e) **FEW**

1. Level One

Exercise 30: 1   Write the 3-letter word that will complete the word in bold type:

Score

1)   A **BY** ball is egg-shaped.   _____

a) **RAP**   b) **RAT**   c) **RAW**   d) **RED**   e) **RUG**

2)   Please don't **SE** the cat.   _____

a) **CAB**   b) **CAN**   c) **CAR**   d) **CAP**   e) **CAT**

3)   Did you see the **FL** of lightning?   _____

a) **ACE**   b) **ASH**   c) **ACT**   d) **AGE**   e) **AGO**

4)   After the fire only **AS** were left.   _____

a) **SAD**   b) **SAG**   c) **SAP**   d) **SHE**   e) **SAT**

5)   **BS** and spices make pasta sauce tastier.   _____

a) **HAD**   b) **HAM**   c) **HAS**   d) **HAT**   e) **HER**

6)   We like to live in **PE** and harmony.   _____

a) **AND**   b) **ACE**   c) **ANT**   d) **APE**   e) **ARC**

7) The **DA** society performed a play. _____

    a) **RIB**   b) **ROB**   c) **RAM**   d) **ROT**   e) **RUN**

8) Our old car went to the **SC** yard. _____

    a) **RAG**   b) **RAM**   c) **RIM**   d) **RAP**   e) **RYE**

9) The wheel fell off the **ON**. _____

    a) **WAG**   b) **WEB**   c) **WHO**   d) **WIN**   e) **WON**

10) I like **GO** chutney with a curry. _____

    a) **MAD**   b) **MID**   c) **MAN**   d) **MOW**   e) **MUG**

11) My **HT** beats faster when I run. _____

    a) **ELF**   b) **EAR**   c) **EVE**   d) **EWE**   e) **EYE**

12) Wholemeal **FL** makes better bread. _____

    a) **OAR**   b) **OFF**   c) **OIL**   d) **OUR**   e) **OAT**

13) I need more **MY** to buy a new game. _____

    a) **OWN**   b) **OUT**   c) **OFF**   d) **ORE**   e) **ONE**

14) The **PI** landed the plane carefully. _____

    a) **LOT**   b) **LEG**   c) **LIT**   d) **LOW**   e) **LAG**

15) We went to the local **TE** park. _____

    a) **HEN**   b) **HIT**   c) **HEM**   d) **HOE**   e) **HUB**

16) It was **DY** on top of the mountain. _____

    a) **WRY**   b) **WIN**   c) **WON**   d) **WIG**   e) **WED**

17) Don't **IC**, stay calm! _____

    a) **PAL**   b) **PEN**   c) **PIP**   d) **PAN**   e) **PUP**

18) We placed the bottles into a **CE**. _____

    a) **RAT**   b) **RIM**   c) **RED**   d) **RAN**   e) **RUG**

19) The **CR** jewels are in the Tower of London. _____

    a) **OAK**   b) **OUR**   c) **OLD**   d) **OWN**   e) **OFT**

20) **SY** beaches are better for walking on. _____

    a) **AID**   b) **AND**   c) **ART**   d) **ASP**   e) **ATE**

2. Level Two

Exercise 30: 2   Write the 3-letter word that will complete the word in bold type: Score

1)   The **FST** fire burned for days. _____

    a) **ORE**   b) **BET**   c) **FED**   d) **HOB**   e) **LIP**

2)   Sand and cement make **MOR**. _____

    a) **VOW**   b) **TEA**   c) **SON**   d) **TAR**   e) **RUE**

3)   She had a **PIA** of spiders. _____

    a) **HOB**   b) **MOB**   c) **NOW**   d) **OWE**   e) **PRY**

4)   The **PIE** stole the ship. _____

    a) **BED**   b) **COG**   c) **AGE**   d) **RAT**   e) **FAR**

5) Can you solve the **DLE**? _____

    a) **LIP**   b) **RID**   c) **HUG**   d) **FIT**   e) **DAY**

6) Help me **SEH** for my keys. _____

    a) **DIE**   b) **CAT**   c) **ARC**   d) **MOB**   e) **LAY**

7) Make some notes in the **MAR**. _____

    a) **RAT**   b) **PEA**   c) **NIL**   d) **LIE**   e) **GIN**

8) I like milk in my **CEE**. _____

    a) **OFF**   b) **BAR**   c) **DIG**   d) **ACE**   e) **GOT**

9) He had a good sense of **OUR**. _____

    a) **FUN**   b) **HUM**   c) **END**   d) **DOE**   e) **PAT**

10) She saved her work on the **LOP**. _____

    a) **NOT**   b) **LAW**   c) **INN**   d) **APT**   e) **ICE**

11) Can I have **AHER** cake, please? _____

    a) **ODD**   b) **NOT**   c) **OPT**   d) **RED**   e) **WIN**

12) A **LEOD** never changes its spots. _____

    a) **PAR**   b) **USE**   c) **PER**   d) **SKI**   e) **SPA**

13) Check your **WORG** out. _____

    a) **RUT**   b) **SAD**   c) **KIN**   d) **COB**   e) **BEE**

14) **IGHT** there will be a full moon. _____

    a) **FLY**   b) **SUN**   c) **BIG**   d) **RYE**   e) **TON**

15) We **ALLY** arrived, after a long journey. _____

    a) **CUE**   b) **GIN**   c) **IVY**   d) **KIT**   e) **FIN**

16) She always won the **ARENT**. _____

    a) **ICE**   b) **GUM**   c) **PEA**   d) **RAG**   e) **OIL**

17) They all **COMED** for the trophy. _____

    a) **LIP**   b) **DIM**   c) **BAY**   d) **PET**   e) **ALE**

18) It is best to always be **THFUL**. _____

    a) **TOE**   b) **RUT**   c) **ROT**   d) **RIM**   e) **LOT**

19) Please do not **UNFAS** your seatbelt. _____

    a) **TOO**   b) **TUG**   c) **SHE**   d) **TEN**   e) **ROT**

20) **PRICE** makes perfect. _____

    a) **SET**   b) **HAD**   c) **FIR**   d) **ACT**   e) **COO**

3. Level Three

Exercise 30: 3   Write the 3-letter word that will complete the word in bold type:

Score

1) Goods are stored in a **WHOUSE**. _____

    a) **ORE**   b) **ARE**   c) **ERA**   d) **SEE**   e) **APE**

2) He **PED** the rose bushes. _____

    a) **POP**   b) **ALL**   c) **ILL**   d) **RUB**   e) **RUN**

3) The police did not **BEVE** his story. _____

    a) **LEA**   b) **EAR**   c) **LIE**   d) **EEL**   e) **LOW**

4) The **MAER** employed more staff. _____

    a) **MAN**   b) **AGE**   c) **NAN**   d) **GUN**   e) **NAG**

5) She said the **RUMS** were untrue. _____

    a) **BAR**   b) **DIM**   c) **OUR**   d) **HUM**   e) **RUE**

6) We **SCD** the mountain. _____

    a) **EEL**   b) **LEG**   c) **ALE**   d) **ORE**   e) **RID**

7) All the class **LISED** to the teacher. _____

    a) **ICE**   b) **ASK**   c) **TON**   d) **TEN**   e) **TIN**

8) Her **SIEL** had long ears. _____

    a) **BIN**   b) **MIT**   c) **PAN**   d) **PIT**   e) **PIN**

9) He put more coal in the **FACE**. _____

    a) **FIR**   b) **HOT**   c) **URN**   d) **CAR**   e) **FAT**

10) It is best to think in a **POIVE** way. _____

    a) **OIL**   b) **POP**   c) **SAT**   d) **TIP**   e) **SIT**

Chapter Thirty-one
LOGICAL REASONING

Each question gives you some information that you need to read in order to work out the answer.

1. Level One

Exercise 31: 1   Work out the answers to the following:

1)   Holly, Linda and Nadia have to be at choir practice by 6.30pm. Nadia is never late. Last week Linda missed the bus and arrived at 6.45pm.

Only one of the following statements must be true: _____

a) Holly is sometimes early for choir practice.
b) Nadia sometimes arrives after Holly.
c) Linda sometimes arrives after Nadia.
d) Holly sometimes arrives before Nadia.
e) Linda always gets the bus to choir practice.

2)   Ramon's father starts work at 8.00am. He had a ten minute break at 10.10am and a fifteen minute break at 2.20pm. He has one hour for lunch and is only paid for the hours he works. How many hours will he be paid for if he finishes work at 4.25pm?   _____

a) 7 hours   b) 7.5 hours   c) 8 hours   d) 6.25 hours   e) 6 hours

3)   Luke lived at number twelve, Omar in flat five and Toby at number eighty. Toby's house had three bedrooms and one bathroom. Omar's home had two bedrooms and two bathrooms. Luke's house had two bathrooms and three bedrooms.

Only one of the following statements must be true: _____

a) Toby had two bedrooms and lived at number eighty.
b) Omar lived in a block of flats in Brighton.
c) Number twelve had two bathrooms.
d) Luke had the largest house.
e) Omar's home had two bedrooms, one bathroom and no stairs.

4) If 'E' is 5 and 'W' is 23 in the alphabet, what is '16'? _____

   a) P   b) Q   c) O   d) R   e) N

5) A garden centre was having a sale of plants. Rose bought a white plant in a red pot. Zara liked the red pot with a white plant. Keri bought a red and white plant in a blue pot, whilst Emma liked the blue and white pot with a red plant.

   Only one of the following statements must be true: _____

   a) Zara liked gardening.
   b) Keri only liked blue pots.
   c) Emma liked the same plant and pot as Keri.
   d) The white plant was bought by Rose.
   e) Zara and Rose liked white plants and pots.

6) Four children were sharing sweets. Mary-Jane had three times as many sweets as Daisy but half as many as Claire. Suzee had five sweets which was two more than Daisy.

   How many more sweets did Mary-Jane have than Suzee? _____

   a) 6   b) 4   c) 3   d) 8   e) 5

7) Three children were sharing a box of marbles. Amber had seven green and four yellow marbles. Jodie had four brown marbles and one with a blue line. Sarah had six brown, one green and three yellow marbles.

   Only one of the following statements must be true: _____

   a) There were eleven marbles altogether.
   b) Sarah had the same number of marbles as Amber.
   c) Only Jodie had a marble with a blue line.
   d) Amber had less marbles than Sarah.
   e) Jodie was Sarah's sister.

8) Beverly is eight years older than Robert. Steven is two years older than Mathew, who is five years younger than Beverly. If Robert is fifteen, how old will Mathew be next year? _____

   a) 19   b) 18   c) 17   d) 20   e) 21

9) Angela's favourite type of potatoes are chips and crisps; Bobby's are mashed and roast. Carl likes crisps but does not like mashed potatoes and Dorothy only likes chips.

   Only one of the following statements must be true: _____

   a) Carl doesn't like chips.
   b) Angela likes chips and mashed potato.
   c) Bobby is the only one who likes mashed potato.
   d) Carl likes mashed potato but not crisps.
   e) Angela likes chips with tomato sauce.

10) Jessica's birthday was on the 27th of January and her party was two weeks later. What was the date of Jessica's party? _____

   a) 8ᵗʰ February   b) 12ᵗʰ February   c) 11ᵗʰ February
   d) 9ᵗʰ February   e) 10ᵗʰ February

11) Alice's dog, Bonnie, had a litter of five pups. Three of the pups were male: two of them were black with white paws and the other was black with a white tip on its tail. One female pup was white with black paws and the other was all black.

   Only one of the following statements must be true: _____

   a) The male pups were all black.
   b) One female pup was all white.
   c) One male pup had two white paws.
   d) One male pup had a white tip on its tail.
   e) The female pups were smaller than the males.

12) The flight time from Liverpool to Gerona is two hours and fifteen minutes. The flight left fifteen minutes late. Spain is one hour ahead of UK time. The flight arrived in Gerona at 11.25am Spanish time.

What time did the flight leave England? _____

a) 9.10am   b) 8.10am   c) 8.20am
d) 7.50am   e) 10.10am

13) Abbie, Brita, Chloe and Daisy were playing in the snow. Abbie was wearing a blue scarf with white stripes and a hat. Brita was wearing a scarf and blue gloves. Chloe was wearing a white scarf with blue stripes and Daisy was wearing a white scarf, hat and gloves.

Only one of the following statements must be true: _____

a) Daisy was wearing least items of winter clothing.
b) Abbie was wearing most items of winter clothing.
c) Daisy and Abbie were friends.
d) Chloe was only wearing a scarf to keep her warm.
e) Brita was wearing white gloves.

14) Anne had a bag of thirty-five sweets. She kept five for herself but gave half of the remaining sweets to Brian and shared the rest equally between Constance, David and Eric.

How many sweets did Brian and David have in total? _____

a) 15   b) 20   c) 10   d) 18   e) 25

15) A teacher was sharing coloured pencils amongst some children in her class. Jared had one red, two blue and four black pencils. Scott had more red pencils than Ellis, but no black or blue pencils. Ellis had four blue, one red and three black pencils.

Only one of the following statements must be true: _____

a) Scott liked red pencils best.
b) Ellis had more red pencils than Jared.
c) Scott had the most red pencils.
d) Jared had more pencils than Ellis.
e) Ellis and Jared were cousins.

16) Zarah went to bed at 8.15pm, Balraj went to bed 20 minutes later and Steven went to bed ten minutes before Zarah.

What time was it 40 minutes before Steven went to bed? _____

a) Twenty-five to eight
b) Twenty-five past seven
c) Twenty past eight
d) Quarter to eight
e) Half past seven

17) Some children lived in a block of four flats. Jack lived in a flat with his two brothers and a sister. Keith lived in flat four with one brother and three sisters whilst Leon lived with his twin brother and older sister. Marcus lived with his baby sister and older brothers.

Only one of the following statements must be true: _____

a) There were four children in Keith's family.
b) Leon's family had two girls.
c) Jack's family had one girl.
d) Marcus's family had two boys and one girl.
e) Jack was the youngest in his family.

18) Jason is five years older than Blair. Ollie is three years older than Rikki, who is three years older than Blair.

If Ollie is sixteen now, how old will Jason be next year? _____

a) 12   b) 13   c) 17   d) 14   e) 16

19) Bristol is south of Gloucester and Worcester is north of Bristol. Gloucester is south of Worcester.

Only one of the following statements must be true: _____

a) Bristol is fifty kilometres from Gloucester.
b) Worcester is north of Bristol and south of Gloucester.
c) Bristol is south of Worcester and north of Gloucester.
d) Gloucester is south of Worcester and Bristol.
e) Gloucester and Bristol are south of Worcester.

20) Matt, Steve and Rob play snooker. Rob pots a red ball followed by the blue ball. Matt pots a red ball, then the green and the white by mistake. Steve pots a red ball followed by the black, then another red followed by the green.

Only one of the following statements must be true: _____

a) Matt and Steve are brothers.
b) Only Matt pots the green ball.
c) Steve and Rob potted the blue ball.
d) The red ball was potted by Matt, Steve and Rob.
e) Steve is definitely the best pool player.

Score

2. Level Two

Exercise 31: 2   Work out the answers to the following:

1)   Bonnie, Blackie, Annie and Bella are black Labradors. Blackie is a male with a curly coat and the others are female. Annie is the smallest and nervous, Bonnie is the oldest and friendly and Bella has a smooth coat and although she is friendly she is also nervous.

Only one of the following statements must be true: _____

a) Annie is the youngest.
b) Blackie is the biggest.
c) Bonnie is the oldest female.
d) Bella is the most nervous.
e) Bonnie and Annie are sisters.

2) Wayne, Tim, Yvonne and Asif collected badges. Wayne had twice as many badges as Tim and two more than Yvonne. Asif had 24 badges; four less than Tim. How many badges did Yvonne and Tim have altogether? _____

a) 82   b) 56   c) 28   d) 72   e) 76

3) Agnieska harvested her vegetables. The peas and beans were collected on the fourth day. The lettuce was picked on the second day. The fennel didn't grow at all but the tomatoes were gathered two days after the peas. Agnieska started to bring in her harvest on Wednesday.

Only one of the following statements must be true: _____

a) The lettuce was picked on Tuesday.
b) The peas were collected two days after the tomatoes.
c) The tomatoes were gathered on Monday.
d) The fennel needed more water before it could grow.
e) The beans were collected on Thursday.

4) Thomas was born in 1996; his sister Edna was born four years earlier and his brother William five years later. How old will Thomas's sister be in 2007? _____

a) 16   b) 15   c) 13   d) 12   e) 17

5) The herbalist sold different teas. Jasmine tea was more popular than green tea, but less popular than raspberry. Raspberry tea was more popular than thyme but less popular than mint tea.

Only one of the following statements must be true: _____

a) Jasmine tea was the most popular.
b) Thyme tea was more popular than green tea.
c) Thyme tea was less popular than any other tea.
d) Mint tea was more popular than any other tea.
e) Raspberry tea was the least popular.

6) If the month before last month was May, what month will it be in three months time? _____

   a) October   b) August   c) July
   d) November   e) September

---

7) Ben, Daisy and Pepe all live together. Ben goes to work during the day and Pepe stays at home with Daisy. Daisy goes shopping on a Friday and Pepe stays with Ben. Sometimes Ben and Daisy go out together and Pepe stays at home. If Ben and Daisy go for a walk Pepe usually goes with them.

   Only one of the following statements must be true: _____

   a) Ben and Daisy like walking.
   b) Pepe doesn't always go out with Ben.
   c) Daisy likes shopping.
   d) Ben doesn't like shopping.
   e) Pepe is a dog.

---

8) Paul, Norris, Freddie, Simon and Ted wear school uniforms. Norris wears a tie, no cap but always wears a jumper and blazer. Simon wears a white shirt, blazer and cap. Paul wears a tie, grey shirt but no blazer. Freddie does not wear a blazer but does wear a tie, jumper and white shirt. Ted wears a cap, tie and grey shirt.

   Who wears least items? _____

   a) Paul   b) Norris   c) Freddie   d) Simon   e) Ted

---

9) What day will it be three days after tomorrow if the day before yesterday was Sunday? _____

   a) Thursday   b) Friday   c) Monday
   d) Sunday   e) Saturday

10) Ricky's uncle, Peter, is five times older than Ricky was the year before last. If Ricky is 12 next year, how old is his uncle now?

   a) 42   b) 40   c) 35   d) 46   e) 45   _____

---

11) Olive trees are harvested in December; almond and cherry trees blossom in April. Orange trees are harvested in March and fig trees do not blossom but are harvested in September.

   Which of the following statements must be true?   _____

   a) Cherry and almond trees are harvested in April.
   b) Orange trees are harvested later in the year than fig trees.
   c) Almond trees blossom in September.
   d) Fig trees are harvested before olive trees.
   e) Orange trees are harvested in December.

---

12) We celebrated Christmas the month before last.
   What month will it be in three months time?   _____

   a) February   b) April   c) March   d) May   e) June

---

13) It usually takes Ken thirty-five minutes to get to the airport, Kyle fifty minutes and Kevin twenty minutes. They need to be at the airport at 5.55am. Kyle arrives five minutes early and Ken arrives ten minutes late.

   Only one of the following statements must be true: _____

   a) Kevin arrives at the airport on time.
   b) Ken arrived at 6.10am.
   c) Kyle always arrives early.
   d) Ken arrived before Kyle.
   e) Ken left home at 5.30am.

---

14) Donald lived with his mum, dad, three sisters and his twin brother. On Friday his younger sister stayed at a friend's house for three nights. Donald's grandmother came to stay for the weekend.

How many people were in Donald's house on Sunday?   _____

a) 3   b) 4   c) 5   d) 6   e) 7

---

15) Smudge, Jet, Elsa, Snowy and Timmy are pet cats.
Elsa, Snowy and Timmy are light coloured cats.
Smudge and Jet have dark fur. Snowy, Timmy and Jet
wear red collars, whilst the other cats wear blue collars.
Elsa and Timmy have short tails.

Only one of the following statements must be true: _____

a) Jet wears a red collar and has a short tail.
b) Snowy has dark fur and wears a blue collar.
c) Smudge and Jet are brother and sister.
d) Jet is the only dark coloured cat that wears a red collar.
e) Elsa is a dark coloured cat with a short tail.

---

16) If E represents Tuesday and N represents Thursday in
the alphabet, what day does W represent?   _____

a) Thursday
b) Monday
c) Friday
d) Wednesday
e) Saturday

---

17) In five years time Javi will be four times older than
Juan was last year. If Javi was fourteen years old last
year, how old is Juan this year?   _____

a) 6   b) 9   c) 7   d) 8   e) 4

---

18) John's birthday is in November, Kay's is three months earlier
and Larry's is five months after Kay's.

What month is two months after Larry's birthday?   _____

a) February   b) March   c) May   d) June   e) April

19) Jack, Kemal and Lynne have bicycles. Jack has a yellow bike with a black stripe and a bell. Kemal has a black bike with red mudguards, caliper brakes but no bell. Lynne's bike is black with yellow handlebars and it is the only one that has twelve gears.

Only one of the following statements must be true: _____

a) Kemal's bike has red mudguards and a bell.
b) Jack has a black bike.
c) Lynne has a yellow bike with a bell.
d) Kemal's is the only bike without mudguards.
e) Lynne's is the only black bike with gears.

20) St. George's day is April 23rd. In 2009 this was on a Thursday. What day was May 5th 2009? _____

a) Sunday   b) Monday   c) Tuesday
d) Wednesday   e) Thursday

Score [ ]

3. Level Three

Exercise 31: 3   Work out the answers to the following:

1) Sabna likes tennis and swimming. Troy likes athletics and tennis. Ulrika likes football and Vernon likes rugby but not athletics. William likes swimming and rugby.

Only one of the following statements must be true: _____

a) William only likes swimming.
b) Ulrika doesn't like athletics.
c) Troy prefers tennis.
d) Three people like swimming.
e) Three sports are equally popular.

2) If the day after tomorrow is 29th October, what will the date be in six days time? _____

a) 5th November   b) 4th November
c) 2nd November   d) 3rd November
e) 6th November

3) Sam, Tim, Tom, Huw and Lee have each bought a house. Tom's house has four bedrooms, two bathrooms and a small garden. Sam and Tim both have three bedrooms and one bathroom, Sam also has a small garden. Huw has one bedroom one bathroom and a large garden. Lee's house has three bedrooms, two bathrooms and no garden.

Only one of the following statements must be true: _____

a) Lee's house has two bedrooms but no garden.
b) Tim's house has three bedrooms and two bathrooms.
c) Tom's house has four bedrooms and a large garden.
d) Sam's house is the only one with three bedrooms and a small garden.
e) Huw has a large garden, two bathrooms and one bedroom.

---

4) Mary-Jane is six years old. In three years time Mary-Jane's nanny, Janet, will be five times Mary-Jane's age.

How old is Janet now? _____

a) 42   b) 40   c) 39   d) 43   e) 44

---

5) There were 20 fish in a tank: six red, eight black and the rest were silver. Four black fish had white markings and all the silver fish had black fins. Two silver and two black fish were then placed into a separate bowl.

Only one of the following statements must be true: _____

a) Only four silver fish had black fins.
b) Two silver and two black fish had white markings.
c) There were four silver fish left in the tank.
d) Four black fish had silver fins.
e) Six red fish had black fins.

---

6) Five children shared out a jar of coloured beads. Alice had twice as many as Alex and half as many as Jake. Toby had twelve beads which was two less than Alex. Zak had two more than Alex.

How many beads did Jake have? _____

a) 60   b) 48   c) 36   d) 28   e) 56

7) A rabbit breeder was taking stock of his rabbits. There were five brown floppy-eared rabbits with white markings, seven white dwarf rabbits with black markings, three albino rabbits that were all white with pink eyes, and four black rabbits with white paws.

Only one of the following statements must be true: _____

a) There were 18 rabbits altogether.
b) The dwarf rabbits were all white.
c) Some rabbits were just one colour with no markings.
d) Four black rabbits had floppy ears.
e) The albino rabbits have black paws.

8) Baby Ruth jumbled up some cards with the first five letters of the alphabet on them. A now came after B but was before C. D came before B but after E and C was last.

Which letter was in the middle? _____

a) A   b) B   c) C   d) D   e) E

9) Joan and her cousins Daisy and Lauren love to read books. Lauren is the fastest reader; she reads 40 pages in one hour. It takes Joan two hours to read the same number of pages. Daisy reads ten more pages per hour than Joan.

How long will it take Daisy to read a book with 150 pages? _____

a) 4 hours   b) 4 hours 30 minutes   c) 5 hours
d) 5 hours 30 minutes   e) 6 hours

10) Five children ate a box of sweets. Claire ate seven sweets, which was four less than Lewis, who ate nine more than Kieran. Miles ate three more than Claire. Gary ate two more than Lewis.

How many sweets were there altogether? _____

a) 45   b) 50   c) 35   d) 37   e) 43   Score

Chapter Thirty-two
SUBSTITUTION

In these questions, letters stand for numbers. Work out the answer to the sums, then choose the correct answer from the options provided.

Example:

> **A = 10, B = 20, C = 30, D = 60** and **E = 80**
>
> What is the answer to this sum written as a letter?
>
> **A + B + C = ?**   Answer ___D___

1. Level One

Exercise 32: 1   Calculate the following: Score

1)   **A = 16, B = 4, C = 12, D = 8** and **E = 24**

What is the answer to this sum written as a letter?

A + C − B = ?   Answer _____

a) **A**   b) **B**   c) **C**   d) **D**   e) **E**

2)   **A = 5, B = 35, C = 3, D = 24** and **E = 4**

What is the answer to this sum written as a letter?

B ÷ A − E = ?   Answer _____

a) **A**   b) **B**   c) **C**   d) **D**   e) **E**

3)   **A = 19, B = 31, C = 24, D = 7** and **E = 12**

What is the answer to this sum written as a letter?

E + A − D = ?   Answer _____

a) **A**   b) **B**   c) **C**   d) **D**   e) **E**

4) **A = 7, B = 2, C = 14, D = 12** and **E = 4**

What is the answer to this sum written as a letter?

$E \times A \div B = ?$ Answer _____

a) **A**   b) **B**   c) **C**   d) **D**   e) **E**

5) **A = 20, B = 37, C = 18, D = 2** and **E = 17**

What is the answer to this sum written as a letter?

$B - C - E = ?$ Answer _____

a) **A**   b) **B**   c) **C**   d) **D**   e) **E**

6) **A = 16, B = 13, C = 26, D = 20** and **E = 29**

What is the answer to this sum written as a letter?

$B + E - A = ?$ Answer _____

a) **A**   b) **B**   c) **C**   d) **D**   e) **E**

7) **A = 46, B = 19, C = 54, D = 27** and **E = 32**

What is the answer to this sum written as a letter?

$C - D + B = ?$ Answer _____

a) **A**   b) **B**   c) **C**   d) **D**   e) **E**

8) **A = 24, B = 48, C = 16, D = 6** and **E = 37**

What is the answer to this sum written as a letter?

$B \div D + C = ?$ Answer _____

a) **A**   b) **B**   c) **C**   d) **D**   e) **E**

9) A = **24**, B = **59**, C = **18**, D = **41** and E = **36**

What is the answer to this sum written as a letter?

B + C – E = ?   Answer _____

a) **A**   b) **B**   c) **C**   d) **D**   e) **E**

10) A = **17**, B = **41**, C = **6**, D = **33** and E = **4**

What is the answer to this sum written as a letter?

C × E + A = ?   Answer _____

a) **A**   b) **B**   c) **C**   d) **D**   e) **E**

11) A = **28**, B = **57**, C = **13**, D = **15** and E = **29**

What is the answer to this sum written as a letter?

B – E – D = ?   Answer _____

a) **A**   b) **B**   c) **C**   d) **D**   e) **E**

12) A = **14**, B = **3**, C = **7**, D = **8** and E = **6**

What is the answer to this sum written as a letter?

C × E ÷ B = ?   Answer _____

a) **A**   b) **B**   c) **C**   d) **D**   e) **E**

13) A = **43**, B = **35**, C = **28**, D = **27** and E = **36**

What is the answer to this sum written as a letter?

A + C – B = ?   Answer _____

a) **A**   b) **B**   c) **C**   d) **D**   e) **E**

14) **A = 39, B = 28, C = 8, D = 21** and **E = 56**

What is the answer to this sum written as a letter?

E ÷ C + D = ?   Answer _____

a) **A**   b) **B**   c) **C**   d) **D**   e) **E**

15) **A = 61, B = 48, C = 0, D = 27** and **E = 34**

What is the answer to this sum written as a letter?

A − E − D = ?   Answer _____

a) **A**   b) **B**   c) **C**   d) **D**   e) **E**

16) **A = 9, B = 5, C = 4, D = 3** and **E = 12**

What is the answer to this sum written as a letter?

C × A ÷ E = ?   Answer _____

a) **A**   b) **B**   c) **C**   d) **D**   e) **E**

17) **A = 54, B = 17, C = 28, D = 15** and **E = 60**

What is the answer to this sum written as a letter?

C + B + D = ?   Answer _____

a) **A**   b) **B**   c) **C**   d) **D**   e) **E**

18) **A = 5, B = 4, C = 47, D = 6** and **E = 17**

What is the answer to this sum written as a letter?

D × A + E = ?   Answer _____

a) **A**   b) **B**   c) **C**   d) **D**   e) **E**

19) **A = 79, B = 56, C = 37, D = 29** and **E = 13**

What is the answer to this sum written as a letter?

C + D + E = ?   Answer _____

a) **A**   b) **B**   c) **C**   d) **D**   e) **E**

20) **A = 42, B = 25, C = 9, D = 63** and **E = 18**

What is the answer to this sum written as a letter?

D ÷ C + E = ?   Answer _____

a) **A**   b) **B**   c) **C**   d) **D**   e) **E**

2. Level Two

Exercise 32: 2   Calculate the following: **Score**

1)   **A = 37, B = 52, C = 81, D = 24** and **E = 17**

What is the answer to this sum written as a letter?

A + D − E + A = ?   Answer _____

a) **A**   b) **B**   c) **C**   d) **D**   e) **E**

2)   **A = 72, B = 27, C = 19, D = 12** and **E = 52**

What is the answer to this sum written as a letter?

A ÷ D + B + C = ?   Answer _____

a) **A**   b) **B**   c) **C**   d) **D**   e) **E**

3)   **A = 32, B = 44, C = 39, D = 17** and **E = 68**

What is the answer to this sum written as a letter?

B + C + D − E = ?   Answer _____

a) **A**   b) **B**   c) **C**   d) **D**   e) **E**

4) **A = 4, B = 9, C = 17, D = 15 and E = 19**

What is the answer to this sum written as a letter?

$A \times B - C - A = ?$ Answer _____

a) **A**   b) **B**   c) **C**   d) **D**   e) **E**

5) **A = 33, B = 7, C = 6, D = 13 and E = 29**

What is the answer to this sum written as a letter?

$B \times B + D - E = ?$ Answer _____

a) **A**   b) **B**   c) **C**   d) **D**   e) **E**

6) **A = 49, B = 24, C = 17, D = 28 and E = 84**

What is the answer to this sum written as a letter?

$E - A + C - D = ?$ Answer _____

a) **A**   b) **B**   c) **C**   d) **D**   e) **E**

7) **A = 56, B = 19, C = 7, D = 18 and E = 9**

What is the answer to this sum written as a letter?

$A \div C + B - E = ?$ Answer _____

a) **A**   b) **B**   c) **C**   d) **D**   e) **E**

8) **A = 42, B = 29, C = 76, D = 34 and E = 63**

What is the answer to this sum written as a letter?

$C - B - D + B = ?$ Answer _____

a) **A**   b) **B**   c) **C**   d) **D**   e) **E**

9) $A = 96$, $B = 58$, $C = 8$, $D = 12$ and $E = 26$

What is the answer to this sum written as a letter?

$A \div C + B + E = ?$ Answer _____

a) A   b) B   c) C   d) D   e) E

10) $A = 35$, $B = 62$, $C = 9$, $D = 36$ and $E = 81$

What is the answer to this sum written as a letter?

$E \div C + B - D = ?$ Answer _____

a) A   b) B   c) C   d) D   e) E

11) $A = 66$, $B = 24$, $C = 8$, $D = 57$ and $E = 39$

What is the answer to this sum written as a letter?

$B \div C + E + B = ?$ Answer _____

a) A   b) B   c) C   d) D   e) E

12) $A = 61$, $B = 70$, $C = 43$, $D = 27$ and $E = 39$

What is the answer to this sum written as a letter?

$E + C + D - E = ?$ Answer _____

a) A   b) B   c) C   d) D   e) E

13) $A = 26$, $B = 7$, $C = 20$, $D = 28$ and $E = 8$

What is the answer to this sum written as a letter?

$B \times E - D - E = ?$ Answer _____

a) A   b) B   c) C   d) D   e) E

14) $A = 5$, $B = 4$, $C = 37$, $D = 55$ and $E = 6$

What is the answer to this sum written as a letter?

$E \times B + C - E = ?$ Answer _____

a) A   b) B   c) C   d) D   e) E

15) $A = 76$, $B = 69$, $C = 38$, $D = 27$ and $E = 23$

What is the answer to this sum written as a letter?

$A - C + E - C = ?$ Answer _____

a) A   b) B   c) C   d) D   e) E

16) $A = 16$, $B = 40$, $C = 38$, $D = 7$ and $E = 63$

What is the answer to this sum written as a letter?

$E \div D + C - D = ?$ Answer _____

a) A   b) B   c) C   d) D   e) E

17) $A = 73$, $B = 97$, $C = 18$, $D = 24$ and $E = 28$

What is the answer to this sum written as a letter?

$B - C - D + C = ?$ Answer _____

a) A   b) B   c) C   d) D   e) E

18) $A = 43$, $B = 32$, $C = 4$, $D = 8$ and $E = 36$

What is the answer to this sum written as a letter?

$B \div D + A - C = ?$ Answer _____

a) A   b) B   c) C   d) D   e) E

19) **A = 47, B = 6, C = 13, D = 7** and **E = 48**

What is the answer to this sum written as a letter?

$D \times B + C - D = ?$ Answer _____

a) **A**   b) **B**   c) **C**   d) **D**   e) **E**

20) **A = 9, B = 12, C = 4, D = 8** and **E = 16**

What is the answer to this sum written as a letter?

$D \times C - E - D = ?$ Answer _____

a) **A**   b) **B**   c) **C**   d) **D**   e) **E**

3. Level Three

Exercise 32: 3   Calculate the following: **Score**

1) **A = 48, B = 12, C = 9, D = 6** and **E = 36**

What is the answer to this sum written as a letter?

$B \times D \div C \times D = ?$ Answer _____

a) **A**   b) **B**   c) **C**   d) **D**   e) **E**

2) **A = 12, B = 135, C = 93, D = 104** and **E = 15**

What is the answer to this sum written as a letter?

$B \div E \times A - E = ?$ Answer _____

a) **A**   b) **B**   c) **C**   d) **D**   e) **E**

3) **A = 13, B = 86, C = 98, D = 12** and **E = 71**

What is the answer to this sum written as a letter?

$D \times A - C + A = ?$ Answer _____

a) **A**   b) **B**   c) **C**   d) **D**   e) **E**

4) **A = 154, B = 22, C = 14, D = 6** and **E = 3**

What is the answer to this sum written as a letter?

$A \div C \times D \div B = ?$ Answer _____

a) **A**   b) **B**   c) **C**   d) **D**   e) **E**

5)   A = 8, B = 6, C = 12, D = 13 and E = 4

What is the answer to this sum written as a letter?

$D \times A \div E - D = ?$ Answer _____

a) A   b) B   c) C   d) D   e) E

6)   A = 98, B = 7, C = 6, D = 12 and E = 86

What is the answer to this sum written as a letter?

$D \times B \div C \times B = ?$ Answer _____

a) A   b) B   c) C   d) D   e) E

7)   A = 63, B = 75, C = 28, D = 48 and E = 15

What is the answer to this sum written as a letter?

$B \div E + C + E = ?$ Answer _____

a) A   b) B   c) C   d) D   e) E

8)   A = 56, B = 54, C = 39, D = 48 and E = 27

What is the answer to this sum written as a letter?

$E + D + E - D = ?$ Answer _____

a) A   b) B   c) C   d) D   e) E

9)   A = 0, B = 6, C = 9, D = 14 and E = 18

What is the answer to this sum written as a letter?

$C \times D \div B \times A = ?$ Answer _____

a) A   b) B   c) C   d) D   e) E

10) A = 87, B = 96, C = 12, D = 16 and E = 108

What is the answer to this sum written as a letter?

$E \div C \times D \div C = ?$ Answer _____

a) A   b) B   c) C   d) D   e) E

Chapter Thirty-three
ARITHMETIC EQUATIONS

In each question, choose the missing number that will complete the question correctly from the options provided.

Example:

$$4 + 2 + 3 = 3 + ?$$

Answer ___6___

1. Level One

Exercise 33: 1   Write the number (not the letter) which will complete the sum:

Score

1) $6 + 7 + 8 = 32 - ?$ Answer _____

     a) **11**   b) **12**   c) **13**   d) **14**   e) **15**

2) $12 + 9 - 8 = 21 - ?$ Answer _____

     a) **4**   b) **5**   c) **6**   d) **7**   e) **8**

3) $17 - 8 + 14 = 6 + ?$ Answer _____

     a) **15**   b) **16**   c) **17**   d) **18**   e) **19**

4) $35 - 9 - 8 = 43 - ?$ Answer _____

     a) **24**   b) **25**   c) **26**   d) **27**   e) **28**

5) $41 + 14 - 18 = 19 + ?$ Answer _____

     a) **15**   b) **16**   c) **17**   d) **18**   e) **19**

6) $13 + 8 + 19 = 22 - 13 + ?$ Answer _____

    a) **28**   b) **29**   c) **30**   d) **31**   e) **32**

7) $23 + 18 - 9 = 25 + 17 - ?$ Answer _____

    a) **6**   b) **7**   c) **8**   d) **9**   e) **10**

8) $44 - 16 + 7 = 17 - 8 + ?$ Answer _____

    a) **26**   b) **27**   c) **28**   d) **29**   e) **30**

9) $39 - 12 - 5 = 45 - 6 - ?$ Answer _____

    a) **16**   b) **17**   c) **18**   d **19**   e) **20**

10) $19 + 23 - 12 = 6 + 9 + ?$ Answer _____

    a) **13**   b) **14**   c) **15**   d) **16**   e) **17**

11) $5 \times 4 - 8 = 6 \times 7 - ?$ Answer _____

    a) **28**   b) **29**   c) **30**   d) **31**   e) **32**

12) $6 \times 3 + 9 = 8 \times 4 - ?$ Answer _____

    a) **4**   b) **5**   c) **6**   d) **7**   e) **8**

13) $7 \times 8 - 16 = 9 \times 3 + ?$ Answer _____

    a) **13**   b) **14**   c) **15**   d) **16**   e) **17**

14) $9 \times 2 + 17 = 7 \times 7 - ?$ Answer _____

     a) **10**   b) **11**   c) **12**   d) **13**   e) **14**

15) $6 \times 6 - 18 = 5 \times 9 - ?$ Answer _____

     a) **24**   b) **25**   c) **26**   d) **27**   e) **28**

16) $9 \times 4 + 15 = 4 \times 7 + ?$ Answer _____

     a) **20**   b) **21**   c) **22**   d) **23**   e) **24**

17) $7 \times 9 - 27 = 8 \times 8 - ?$ Answer _____

     a) **28**   b) **29**   c) **30**   d) **31**   e) **32**

18) $3 \times 4 \times 5 = 9 \times 7 - ?$ Answer _____

     a) **7**   b) **6**   c) **5**   d) **4**   e) **3**

19) $2 \times 6 \times 7 = 9 \times 9 + ?$ Answer _____

     a) **2**   b) **3**   c) **4**   d) **5**   e) **6**

20) $3 \times 6 \times 2 = 6 \times 7 - ?$ Answer _____

     a) **4**   b) **5**   c) **6**   d) **7**   e) **8**

2. Level Two

Exercise 33: 2   Write the number (not the letter) which will complete the sum: **Score**

1) $23 + 18 - 12 = 43 - 27 + ?$ Answer _____

    a) **13**   b) **14**   c) **15**   d) **16**   e) **17**

2) $6 \times 7 + 19 = 12 \times 4 + ?$ Answer _____

    a) **9**   b) **10**   c) **11**   d) **12**   e) **13**

3) $54 \div 9 + 24 = 56 \div 8 + ?$ Answer _____

    a) **21**   b) **22**   c) **23**   d) **24**   e) **25**

4) $72 \div 6 - 12 = 81 \div 9 - ?$ Answer _____

    a) **6**   b) **7**   c) **8**   d) **9**   e) **10**

5) $61 - 17 - 22 = 73 - 19 - ?$ Answer _____

    a) **32**   b) **33**   c) **34**   d) **35**   e) **36**

6) $8 \times 8 - 18 = 7 \times 7 - ?$ Answer _____

    a) **0**   b) **1**   c) **2**   d) **3**   e) **4**

7) $17 + 18 + 25 = 36 + 45 - ?$ Answer _____

    a) **19**   b) **20**   c) **21**   d) **22**   e) **23**

8) $64 \div 8 \times 7 = 7 \times 4 \times \,?$ Answer _____

   a) **6**   b) **5**   c) **4**   d) **3**   e) **2**

9) $9 \times 3 \times 2 = 18 \div 2 \times \,?$ Answer _____

   a) **5**   b) **6**   c) **7**   d) **8**   e) **9**

10) $79 - 21 - 29 = 54 + 37 - \,?$ Answer _____

   a) **60**   b) **61**   c) **62**   d) **63**   e) **64**

11) $56 \div 8 + 33 = 49 \div 7 + \,?$ Answer _____

   a) **33**   b) **38**   c) **39**   d) **40**   e) **41**

12) $63 \div 7 - 9 = 121 \div 11 - \,?$ Answer _____

   a) **8**   b) **9**   c) **10**   d) **11**   e) **12**

13) $73 - 19 - 27 = 63 - 29 - \,?$ Answer _____

   a) **6**   b) **7**   c) **8**   d) **9**   e) **10**

14) $7 \times 8 - 38 = 6 \times 6 - \,?$ Answer _____

   a) **14**   b) **15**   c) **16**   d) **17**   e) **18**

15) $23 + 19 + 32 = 53 + 37 - \,?$ Answer _____

   a) **12**   b) **13**   c) **14**   d) **15**   e) **16**

16) $54 \div 6 \times 7 = 7 \times 3 \times$ **?**   Answer _____

    a) **3**   b) **4**   c) **5**   d) **6**   e) **7**

17) $8 \times 4 \times 2 = 72 \div 9 \times$ **?**   Answer _____

    a) **5**   b) **6**   c) **7**   d) **8**   e) **9**

18) $81 - 33 - 18 = 61 + 29 -$ **?**   Answer _____

    a) **59**   b) **60**   c) **61**   d) **62**   e) **63**

19) $96 \div 8 + 12 = 84 \div 7 +$ **?**   Answer _____

    a) **10**   b) **11**   c) **12**   d) **13**   e) **14**

20) $15 \times 4 - 28 = 16 \times 3 -$ **?**   Answer _____

    a) **16**   b) **17**   c) **18**   d) **19**   e) **20**

3. Level Three

Exercise 33: 3   Write the number (not the letter) which will complete the sum: Score

1) $13 \times 4 + 18 = 16 \times 5 -$ **?**   Answer _____

    a) **8**   b) **9**   c) **10**   d) **11**   e) **12**

2) $132 \div 4 + 17 = 108 \div 6 +$ **?**   Answer _____

    a) **29**   b) **30**   c) **31**   d) **32**   e) **33**

3) $14 \times 4 - 28 = 84 \div ?$ Answer _____

a) **1**   b) **2**   c) **3**   d) **4**   e) **5**

4) $168 \div 14 = 36 \times 4 \div ?$ Answer _____

a) **11**   b) **12**   c) **13**   d) **14**   e) **15**

5) $17 \times 3 + 19 = 28 \div 2 \times ?$ Answer _____

a) **2**   b) **3**   c) **4**   d) **5**   e) **6**

6) $6 \times 7 \times 3 = 14 \times ?$ Answer _____

a) **9**   b) **10**   c) **11**   d) **12**   e) **13**

7) $108 \div 6 \times 3 = 16 \times 5 - ?$ Answer _____

a) **24**   b) **25**   c) **26**   d) **27**   e) **28**

8) $56 \div 8 \times 7 = 84 \div 12 \times ?$ Answer _____

a) **3**   b) **4**   c) **5**   d) **6**   e) **7**

9) $17 \times 8 = 9 \times 12 + ?$ Answer _____

a) **25**   b) **26**   c) **27**   d) **28**   e) **29**

10) $8 \times 8 - 35 = 174 \div ?$ Answer _____

a) **4**   b) **5**   c) **6**   d) **7**   e) **8**

Chapter Thirty-four
NUMBER SEQUENCING

In each question, choose the next number in the sequence from the options provided.

Example:

4, 6, 8, 10, ?   Answer __12__

1. Level One

Exercise 34: 1   Write the next number in the sequence:

Score

1) **6, 3, 8, 5, 10, ?**   Answer _____

   a) **2**   b) **5**   c) **6**   d) **7**   e) **8**

2) **18, 50, 21, 57, 24, ?**   Answer _____

   a) **55**   b) **64**   c) **27**   d) **29**   e) **60**

3) **15, 19, 25, 29, 35, 39, ?**   Answer _____

   a) **45**   b) **44**   c) **46**   d) **48**   e) **49**

4) **31, 25, 20, 16, 13, ?**   Answer _____

   a) **15**   b) **14**   c) **13**   d) **12**   e) **11**

5) **12, 7, 14, 9, 17, 12, ?**   Answer _____

   a) **22**   b) **18**   c) **23**   d) **20**   e) **21**

6) **21, 15, 17, 19, 13, 23, ?**   Answer _____

   a) **7**   b) **9**   c) **13**   d) **19**   e) **10**

7) **27, 18, 24, 22, 21, 26, ?**   Answer _____

    a) **27**   b) **18**   c) **19**   d) **17**   e) **20**

8) **32, 33, 35, 38, 42, 47, ?**   Answer _____

    a) **50**   b) **33**   c) **38**   d) **47**   e) **53**

9) **7, 14, 10, 17, 13, 20, ?**   Answer _____

    a) **15**   b) **20**   c) **16**   d) **17**   e) **19**

10) **29, 32, 36, 39, 43, 46, ?**   Answer _____

    a) **40**   b) **50**   c) **44**   d) **54**   e) **45**

11) **48, 43, 41, 36, 34, 29, ?**   Answer _____

    a) **27**   b) **25**   c) **20**   d) **23**   e) **24**

12) **7, 13, 11, 17, 16, 22, ?**   Answer _____

    a) **22**   b) **21**   c) **19**   d) **18**   e) **24**

13) **21, 11, 16, 15, 11, 19, ?**   Answer _____

    a) **44**   b) **2**   c) **5**   d) **7**   e) **6**

14) **32, 49, 38, 43, 44, 37, ?**   Answer _____

    a) **49** b) **51** c) **48**   d) **50**   e) **52**

15) **61, 38, 57, 44, 53, 50, ?**   Answer _____

    a) **48**   b) **51**   c) **49**   d) **47**   e) **52**

16) **54, 50, 47, 47, 40, 44, ?**   Answer _____

    a) **31**   b) **33**   c) **35**   d) **32**   e) **37**

17) **3, 7, 15, 27, ?**   Answer _____

    a) **43**   b) **45**   c) **52**   d) **42**   e) **15**

18) **47, 44, 38, 29, ?**   Answer _____

    a) **15**   b) **18**   c) **16**   d) **17**   e) **19**

19) **61, 43, 28, 16, ?**   Answer _____

    a) **1**   b) **5**   c) **4**   d) **7**   e) **9**

20) **7, 8, 11, 16, 23, ?**   Answer _____

    a) **24**   b) **18**   c) **30**   d) **36**   e) **32**

2. Level Two

Exercise 34: 2   Write the next number in the sequence:

Score

1) **16, 17, 19, 22, 23, 25, ?**   Answer _____

    a) **26**   b) **23**   c) **28**   d) **30**   e) **29**

2) **41, 38, 36, 35, 32, 30, ?**   Answer _____

    a) **30**   b) **28**   c) **29**   d) **38**   e) **32**

3) **21, 23, 27, 33, 35, 39, ?**   Answer _____

    a) **45**   b) **38**   c) **46**   d) **50**   e) **41**

4) **50**, **42**, **38**, **36**, **28**, **24**, **?** Answer _____

   a) **26**   b) **24**   c) **28**   d) **22**   e) **36**

5) **7**, **10**, **16**, **25**, **28**, **34**, **?** Answer _____

   a) **43**   b) **42**   c) **45**   d) **25**   e) **36**

6) **44**, **38**, **34**, **32**, **26**, **22**, **?** Answer _____

   a) **18**   b) **21**   c) **19**   d) **20**   e) **17**

7) **35**, **32**, **34**, **33**, **30**, **32**, **?** Answer _____

   a) **19**   b) **35**   c) **32**   d) **31**   e) **30**

8) **6**, **8**, **5**, **9**, **11**, **8**, **?** Answer _____

   a) **10**   b) **9**   c) **13**   d) **8**   e) **12**

9) **2**, **4**, **0**, **6**, **8**, **4**, **?** Answer _____

   a) **10**   b) **6**   c) **8**   d) **12**   e) **9**

10) **6**, **32**, **12**, **16**, **24**, **8**, **?** Answer _____

   a) **40**   b) **48**   c) **46**   d) **44**   e) **47**

11) **0**, **1**, **1**, **2**, **3**, **?** Answer _____

   a) **4**   b) **1**   c) **5**   d) **2**   e) **0**

12) **2**, **9**, **6**, **18**, **18**, **27**, **?** Answer _____

   a) **45**   b) **52**   c) **54**   d) **55**   e) **48**

13) **13, 17, 25, 41, ?**　　　Answer _____

　　a) **70**　b) **54**　c) **73**　d) **75**　e) **51**

14) **4, 1, 8, 3, 16, 9, 32, ?**　　　Answer _____

　　a) **27**　b) **36**　c) **18**　d) **29**　e) **40**

15) **49, 33, 25, 21, ?**　　　Answer _____

　　a) **15**　b) **18**　c) **17**　d) **14**　e) **19**

16) **48, 24, 12, 6, ?**　　　Answer _____

　　a) **1**　b) **3**　c) **4**　d) **5**　e) **2**

17) **102, 94, 88, 84, 76, 70, ?**　　　Answer _____

　　a) **66**　b) **64**　c) **68**　d) **67**　e) **65**

18) **91, 14, 84, 28, 77, 56, 70, ?**　　　Answer _____

　　a) **63**　b) **112**　c) **61**　d) **121**　e) **113**

19) **4, 4, 8, 12, 16, 20, ?**　　　Answer _____

　　a) **16**　b) **20**　c) **36**　d) **38**　e) **32**

20) **7, 14, 16, 32, 34, ?**　　　Answer _____

　　a) **60**　b) **66**　c) **70**　d) **68**　e) **72**

3. Level Three

Score

Exercise 34: 3　Write the next number in the sequence:

1) **4, 10, 22, 46, ?**　　　Answer _____

　　a) **96**　b) **112**　c) **90**　d) **94**　e) **44**

2) **116, 114, 38, 36, 12, ?**   Answer _____

    a) **9**   b) **8**   c) **10**   d) **6**   e) **3**

3) **2, 3, 5, 7, 11, ?**   Answer _____

    a) **14**   b) **13**   c) **12**   d) **16**   e) **17**

4) **7, 16, 32, 57, ?**   Answer _____

    a) **93**   b) **90**   c) **99**   d) **95**   e) **102**

5) **480, 96, 24, 8, 4, ?**   Answer _____

    a) **12**   b) **0**   c) **4**   d) **1**   e) **2**

6) **3, 3, 6, 18, 72, ?**   Answer _____

    a) **90**   b) **120**   c) **144**   d) **200**   e) **360**

7) **17, 18, 18, 17, 15, ?**   Answer _____

    a) **20**   b) **17**   c) **12**   d) **16**   e) **14**

8) **4, 8, 9, 27, 16, 64, 25, ?**   Answer _____

    a) **125**   b) **100**   c) **128**   d) **150**   e) **130**

9) **81, 100, 121, 144, 169, ?**   Answer _____

    a) **190**   b) **225**   c) **196**   d) **200**   e) **192**

10) **7, 8, 15, 23, 38, ?**   Answer _____

    a) **76**   b) **61**   c) **54**   d) **72**   e) **80**

Chapter Thirty-five
NUMBER LINKS

In these questions, the middle number in the last group is made up in the same way as the middle number in the first two groups. Write the missing number.

Example:

(3 [7] 4) (6 [8] 2)

(6 [?] 5)   _11_

1. Level One

Exercise 35: 1   Write the missing number: Score

1)   (23 [16] 9) (17 [10] 3)

(34 [?] 20)   Answer _____

   a) **25**   b) **28**   c) **27**   d) **26**   e) **29**

2)   (36 [4] 9) (28 [4] 7)

(64 [?] 8)   Answer _____

   a) **1**   b) **6**   c) **15**   d) **8**   e) **9**

3)   (21 [34] 13) (19 [36] 17)

(32 [?] 29)   Answer _____

   a) **61**   b) **53**   c) **59**   d) **62**   e) **63**

4)   (5 [15] 45) (7 [21] 63)

(6 [?] 54)   Answer _____

   a) **18**   b) **16**   c) **14**   d) **20**   e) **19**

5) (47 [28] 19)   (53 [26] 27)
   (72 [?] 28)   Answer _____

   a) 38   b) 44   c) 41   d) 42   e) 40

6) (30 [42] 54)   (12 [24] 36)
   (17 [?] 41)   Answer _____

   a) 27   b) 24   c) 30   d) 31   e) 29

7) (64 [8] 8)   (63 [7] 9)
   (60 [?] 5)   Answer _____

   a) 11   b) 9   c) 12   d) 15   e) 8

8) (17 [42] 25)   (23 [72] 49)
   (57 [?] 27)   Answer _____

   a) 84   b) 82   c) 85   d) 78   e) 83

9) (32 [8] 4)   (16 [8] 2)
   (48 [?] 3)   Answer _____

   a) 14   b) 24   c) 16   d) 12   e) 20

10) (7 [56] 8)   (9 [54] 6)
    (12 [?] 7)   Answer _____

    a) 67   b) 84   c) 72   d) 85   e) 73

11) (38 [58] 96)   (76 [29] 105)
    (89 [?] 124)   Answer _____

    a) 34   b) 33   c) 37   d) 35   e) 36

12) **(72 [9] 8)   (30 [6] 5)**
       (49 [?] 7)   Answer _____

    a) **2**   b) **9**   c) **5**   d) **8**   e) **7**

13) **(12 [48] 4)   (4 [28] 7)**
       (6 [?] 9)   Answer _____

    a) **45**   b) **37**   c) **54**   d) **63**   e) **29**

14) **(89 [134] 45)   (32 [101] 69)**
       (65 [?] 77)   Answer _____

    a) **143**   b) **142**   c) **140**   d) **139**   e) **141**

15) **(36 [6] 6)   (55 [5] 11)**
       (63 [?] 9)   Answer _____

    a) **3**   b) **9**   c) **6**   d) **8**   e) **7**

16) **(81 [9] 9)   (84 [7] 12)**
       (56 [?] 7)   Answer _____

    a) **5**   b) **7**   c) **8**   d) **6**   e) **9**

17) **(64 [27] 37)   (76 [57] 19)**
       (92 [?] 68)   Answer _____

    a) **22**   b) **23**   c) **27**   d) **24**   e) **26**

18) **(72 [6] 12)   (56 [7] 8)**
       (132 [?] 12)   Answer _____

    a) **6**   b) **11**   c) **8**   d) **9**   e) **12**

19) (12 [96] 8)   (9 [63] 7)
(12 [?] 14)   Answer _____

a) 162   b) 164   c) 168   d) 158   e) 156

20) (78 [27] 105)   (87 [29] 116)
(89 [?] 138)   Answer _____

a) 48   b) 47   c) 51   d) 50   e) 49

2. Level Two

Exercise 35: 2 Write the missing number:

Score

1)   (9 [25] 7)   (8 [22] 6)
(7 [?] 11)   Answer _____

a) 25   b) 52   c) 35   d) 53   e) 45

2)   (6 [16] 5)   (7 [15] 4)
(8 [?] 6)   Answer _____

a) 18   b) 20   c) 22   d) 16   e) 24

3)   (21 [30] 6)   (17 [18] 8)
(18 [?] 9)   Answer _____

a) 24   b) 16   c) 26   d) 18   e) 20

4)   (3 [42] 7)   (5 [40] 4)
(6 [?] 8)   Answer _____

a) 72   b) 83   c) 64   d) 96   e) 69

5) (36 [12] 9) (28 [21] 4)
    (42 [?] 7)   Answer _____

   a) 16   b) 18   c) 12   d) 14   e) 20

6) (16 [12] 8) (18 [15] 12)
    (24 [?] 18)   Answer _____

   a) 20   b) 23   c) 19   d) 25   e) 21

7) (17 [3] 8) (21 [4] 9)
    (24 [?] 6)   Answer _____

   a) 4   b) 3   c) 6   d) 2   e) 5

8) (8 [23] 7) (9 [31] 13)
    (6 [?] 15)   Answer _____

   a) 20   b) 29   c) 35   d) 30   e) 27

9) (7 [19] 9) (8 [25] 14)
    (11 [?] 13)   Answer _____

   a) 25   b) 29   c) 26   d) 27   e) 24

10) (23 [80] 7) (21 [75] 6)
    (27 [?] 9)   Answer _____

   a) 86   b) 90   c) 92   d) 84   e) 72

11) (4 [18] 5) (9 [52] 6)
    (9 [?] 12)   Answer _____

   a) 98   b) 102   c) 104   d) 100   e) 106

12) **(32 [2] 8) (49 [5] 7)**
(48 [?] 6)   Answer _____

a) **4**   b) **5**   c) **6**   d) **8**   e) **7**

13) **(13 [6] 17) (16 [5] 9)**
(15 [?] 25)   Answer _____

a) **9**   b) **7**   c) **12**   d) **8**   e) **13**

14) **(18 [3] 6) (23 [4] 7)**
(24 [?] 4)   Answer _____

a) **7**   b) **8**   c) **6**   d) **9**   e) **5**

15) **(6 [25] 9) (7 [22] 5)**
(8 [?] 12)   Answer _____

a) **26**   b) **29**   c) **28**   d) **27**   e) **30**

16) **(8 [28] 6) (12 [38] 7)**
(9 [?] 11)   Answer _____

a) **30**   b) **52**   c) **50**   d) **41**   e) **40**

17) **(25 [15] 6) (34 [23] 7)**
(26 [?] 8)   Answer _____

a) **11**   b) **10**   c) **13**   d) **12**   e) **14**

18) **(6 [19] 4) (7 [16] 3)**
(8 [?] 5)   Answer _____

a) **35**   b) **39**   c) **36**   d) **34**   e) **32**

19)   (30 [24] 5)   (24 [12] 8)
        (36 [?] 9)   Answer _____

   a) 8   b) 12   c) 18   d) 14   e) 16

20)   (16 [10] 14)   (15 [7] 6)
        (21 [?] 12)   Answer _____

   a) 13   b) 10   c) 8   d) 11   e) 12

3. Level Three

Score

Exercise 35: 3   Write the missing number:

1)   (25 [5] 7)   (24 [4] 8)
        (42 [?] 5)   Answer _____

   a) 13   b) 14   c) 15   d) 16   e) 17

2)   (4 [36] 3)   (6 [90] 5)
        (16 [?] 2)   Answer _____

   a) 86   b) 94   c) 96   d) 92   e) 83

3)   (3 [45] 9)   (7 [108] 12)
        (11 [?] 13)   Answer _____

   a) 143   b) 170   c) 156   d) 182   e) 169

4)   (57 [3] 21)   (84 [4] 23)
        (126 [?] 20)   Answer _____

   a) 5   b) 9   c) 7   d) 8   e) 6

5) (4 [160] 80)   (6 [96] 32)
        (5 [?] 62)   Answer _____

   a) 150   b) 155   c) 158   d) 142   e) 145

6) (36 [44] 4)   (30 [40] 5)
        (40 [?] 8)   Answer _____

   a) 48   b) 54   c) 56   d) 58   e) 60

7) (54 [12] 6)   (72 [14] 10)
        (93 [?] 11)   Answer _____

   a) 16   b) 18   c) 24   d) 20   e) 22

8) (4 [28] 11)   (6 [36] 13)
        (7 [?] 15)   Answer _____

   a) 44   b) 46   c) 38   d) 40   e) 42

9) (6 [55] 65)   (14 [72] 90)
        (23 [?] 84)   Answer _____

   a) 60   b) 57   c) 59   d) 58   e) 61

10) (4 [39] 3)   (3 [48] 5)
        (8 [?] 4)   Answer _____

   a) 97   b) 98   c) 99   d) 96   e) 95

Answers

Chapter Twenty-six
Similar Meanings
Exercise 26: 1

1) mend   repair
2) goal   aim
3) link   bond
4) heap   stack
5) same   alike
6) over   above
7) arch   curve
8) gain   grow
9) fall   drop
10) zero   nil
11) swat   hit
12) help   aid
13) pick   reap
14) knot   bind
15) hero   idol
16) lack   need
17) risk   danger
18) actual   real
19) tale   story
20) solo   alone

Exercise 26: 2

1) brave   bold
2) messy   chaotic
3) typical   usual
4) whine   complain
5) wilt   droop
6) nudge   bump
7) recite   narrate
8) faith   belief
9) plant   sow
10) cancel   stop
11) gadget   device
12) chorus   choir
13) wreck   ruin
14) chute   slide
15) midst   middle
16) unify   merge
17) theme   topic
18) ability   talent
19) energy   force
20) dismay   shock

Exercise 26: 3

1) debris   rubble
2) patient   tolerant
3) scene   vista
4) measure   gauge
5) possible   probable
6) significant   important
7) tyrant   dictator
8) courteous   cordial
9) jealous   envious
10) fragrant   aromatic

Chapter Twenty-seven
Word Links
Exercise 27: 1

1) nippy
2) pinch
3) farm
4) house
5) star
6) fasten
7) grant
8) spot
9) print
10) further
11) juice
12) key
13) job
14) break
15) pick
16) shade
17) sort
18) track
19) fair
20) fine

Exercise 27: 2

1) retreat
2) exploit
3) strike
4) puzzle
5) uniform
6) plan
7) present
8) reserve
9) life
10) deal
11) sink
12) throw
13) endure
14) study
15) block
16) mean
17) pitch
18) object
19) force
20) equal

Exercise 27: 3

1) hide
2) monitor
3) market
4) flag
5) display
6) submit
7) hole
8) tender
9) shape
10) tack

Chapter Twenty-eight
Opposite Meanings
Exercise 28: 1

1) alike   different
2) frail   strong
3) fluid   solid
4) melt   freeze
5) bald   hairy
6) inner   outer
7) worst   best

Answers

8) plain fancy
9) clean soiled
10) push pull
11) rage calm
12) pause continue
13) rapid slow
14) decline accept
15) hold release
16) rough soft
17) fact fiction
18) wrong correct
19) level uneven
20) divide join

Exercise 28: 2
1) bland spicy
2) acknowledge ignore
3) flawed perfect
4) excess shortage
5) vacant occupied
6) enrage console
7) thrive deteriorate
8) direct winding
9) forget recall
10) bold shy
11) trivial important
12) upset comfort
13) general specific
14) scarce abundant
15) humble arrogant
16) bored interested
17) upright horizontal
18) clear opaque
19) cautious reckless
20) gorge starve

Exercise 28: 3
1) placate irritate
2) merge detach
3) developed primitive
4) pure contaminated
5) diminish escalate

6) discard retain
7) mundane exceptional
8) refrain persist
9) solitary sociable
10) hoard jettison

Chapter Twenty-nine
Odd Ones Out
Exercise 29: 1
1) apple fruit
2) transport travel
3) council visit
4) climb higher
5) joint body
6) fuel liquid
7) sport compete
8) shape sign
9) crossing bird
10) drink racquet
11) hat coat
12) knife farm
13) feel sweet
14) mouse thimble
15) cloud weather
16) union league
17) shell cave
18) room space
19) float swim
20) lords survey

Exercise 29: 2
1) festival deliver
2) country pelican
3) weaken kick
4) ruler regatta
5) shorts shoes
6) chop bore
7) sign site
8) swede leek
9) stop go
10) train power
11) mortice strong

12) collect yearly
13) cygnet owlet
14) raspberry grape
15) channel belong
16) world dice
17) celebrity starlet
18) knife hair
19) jacket blazer
20) hedge garden

Exercise 29: 3
1) touch sense
2) swift hasty
3) trout banana
4) octopus shark
5) canal accurate
6) decay ample
7) summit oasis
8) cabbage pumpkin
9) direct almost
10) imitate pretend

Chapter Thirty
Missing Words
Exercise 30: 1
1) RUG
2) CAR
3) ASH
4) SHE
5) HER
6) ACE
7) RAM
8) RAP
9) WAG
10) MAN
11) EAR
12) OUR
13) ONE
14) LOT
15) HEM
16) WIN
17) PAN

Answers

18) RAT
19) OWN
20) AND

Exercise 30: 2
1) ORE
2) TAR
3) HOB
4) RAT
5) RID
6) ARC
7) GIN
8) OFF
9) HUM
10) APT
11) NOT
12) PAR
13) KIN
14) TON
15) FIN
16) GUM
17) PET
18) RUT
19) TEN
20) ACT

Exercise 30: 3
1) ARE
2) RUN
3) LIE
4) NAG
5) OUR
6) ALE
7) TEN
8) PAN
9) URN
10) SIT

Chapter Thirty-one
Logical Reasoning
Exercise 31: 1
1) c

2) a
3) c
4) a
5) d
6) b
7) c
8) a
9) c
10) e
11) d
12) b
13) d
14) b
15) c
16) b
17) c
18) e
19) e
20) d

Exercise 31: 2
1) c
2) a
3) c
4) b
5) d
6) a
7) b
8) a
9) e
10) e
11) d
12) d
13) e
14) e
15) d
16) e
17) a
18) b
19) e
20) c

Exercise 31: 3
1) e
2) c
3) d
4) a
5) c
6) e
7) c
8) b
9) c
10) e

Chapter Thirty-two
Substitution
Exercise 32: 1
1) E
2) C
3) C
4) C
5) D
6) C
7) A
8) A
9) D
10) B
11) C
12) A
13) E
14) B
15) C
16) D
17) E
18) C
19) A
20) B

Exercise 32: 2
1) C
2) E
3) A
4) D
5) A

6) B
7) D
8) A
9) A
10) A
11) A
12) B
13) C
14) D
15) E
16) B
17) A
18) A
19) E
20) D

Exercise 32: 3
1) A
2) C
3) E
4) E
5) D
6) A
7) D
8) B
9) A
10) C

Chapter Thirty-three
Arithmetic Equations
Exercise 33: 1
1) 11
2) 8
3) 17
4) 25
5) 18
6) 31
7) 10
8) 26
9) 17

Answers

10) 15
11) 30
12) 5
13) 13
14) 14
15) 27
16) 23
17) 28
18) 3
19) 3
20) 6

Exercise 33: 2
1) 13
2) 13
3) 23
4) 9
5) 32
6) 3
7) 21
8) 2
9) 6
10) 62
11) 33
12) 11
13) 7
14) 18
15) 16
16) 3
17) 8
18) 60
19) 12
20) 16

Exercise 33: 3
1) 10
2) 32
3) 3
4) 12
5) 5
6) 9
7) 26

8) 7
9) 28
10) 6

Chapter Thirty-four
Number Sequencing
Exercise 34: 1
1) 7
2) 64
3) 45
4) 11
5) 21
6) 9
7) 18
8) 53
9) 16
10) 50
11) 27
12) 22
13) 6
14) 50
15) 49
16) 33
17) 43
18) 17
19) 7
20) 32

Exercise 34: 2
1) 28
2) 29
3) 45
4) 22
5) 43
6) 20
7) 31
8) 12
9) 10
10) 48
11) 5

12) 54
13) 73
14) 27
15) 19
16) 3
17) 66
18) 112
19) 32
20) 68

Exercise 34: 3
1) 94
2) 10
3) 13
4) 93
5) 4
6) 360
7) 12
8) 125
9) 196
10) 61

Chapter Thirty-five
Number Links
Exercise 35: 1
1) 27
2) 8
3) 61
4) 18
5) 44
6) 29
7) 12
8) 84
9) 16
10) 84
11) 35
12) 7
13) 54
14) 142
15) 7
16) 8
17) 24

18) 11
19) 168
20) 49

Exercise 35: 2
1) 25
2) 20
3) 18
4) 96
5) 18
6) 21
7) 6
8) 27
9) 27
10) 90
11) 106
12) 6
13) 8
14) 5
15) 30
16) 40
17) 14
18) 35
19) 16
20) 11

Exercise 35: 3
1) 14
2) 96
3) 169
4) 7
5) 155
6) 56
7) 20
8) 42
9) 57
10) 99

PROGRESS CHARTS

Exercise	Score	Total Score	%
26: 1			
26: 2			
26: 3			
27: 1			
27: 2			
27: 3			
28: 1			
28: 2			
28: 3			
29: 1			
29: 2			
29: 3			
30: 1			
30: 2			
30: 3			

Exercise	Score	Total Score	%
31: 1			
31: 2			
31: 3			
32: 1			
32: 2			
32: 3			
33: 1			
33: 2			
33: 3			
34: 1			
34: 2			
34: 3			
35: 1			
35: 2			
35: 3			

Overall Score	Overall Percentage
	%

© 2011 Stephen Curran

CERTIFICATE OF

ACHIEVEMENT

This certifies

_____

has successfully completed

11+ Verbal Reasoning
Year 5-7 GL & Other Styles
WORKBOOK **5**

Overall percentage
score achieved ⬚ **%**

Comment _____

_____

Signed _____
(teacher/parent/guardian)

Date _____